May 31st 1989

Happy Birthday
To T.J.

Love Mom.

How to Speak Cat

Also by the Author

The Begin Note's Role in Meaning

A Preliminary Grammar of Cat

Tonality in Spoken Cat

Cat Grammar

Thus Spake Zarathustra's Cat

HOW TO
SPEAK CAT

The Essential Primer of
Cat Language

Alexandra Sellers

HarperCollins*Publishers*

HarperCollins books may be purchased for educational, business, or sales promotional use. For information please write: Special Markets Department, HarperCollins Publishers, Inc., 10 East 53rd Street, New York, NY 10022.

FIRST EDITION

Designed by Interrobang Design Studio

Library of Congress Cataloging-in-Publication Data
Sellers, Alexandra.
[Spoken Cat]
How to speak Cat : the essential primer of Cat language / by Alexandra Sellers. — 1st ed.
p.   cm.
Published in the UK in 1997 by Bellew under the title: Spoken Cat.
ISBN 0-06-017545-1
1. Cats—Behavior.   2. Animal communication.   3. Human-animal communication.   4. Animal sounds.   I. Title.
SF446.5.S45   1998
636.8—dc21   97–41541

98 99 00 01 02 ❖/RRD 10 9 8 7 6 5 4 3 2

to
The One Who
IS
… shall I play for you?

It is manifestly evident that there is among them a full and entire communication, and that they understand each other.

MICHEL DE MONTAIGNE

Contents

TONALITY

Acknowledgments

Many individuals, both feline and human, helped in the writing of this book. My thanks in particular go to Johnny, Medico, Mickey, Rufus, Fluffy, Pussum, Puffin, Floyd, Beetle, and Prickles for their (nearly) endless patience and their heroic efforts to stick to the truth. Without them, nothing could have been achieved. My grateful thanks also to Dr. Leigh Lisker at the University of Pennsylvania, who read the manuscript and made many helpful suggestions, to Dr. Alexander McKay at the International Institute in Leiden, who was always a source of scholarly advice, and to Ib Bellew of Bellew Publishing.

Thanks to Harcourt Brace and Company for permission to quote from *Old Possum's Book of Practical Cats* by T. S. Eliot. I have used the 1982 edition.

Introduction

The language of Cats[1] is as old as what humans call "the domestiCation of the Cat" (Cats give it quite a different name), doubtless much older, and has survived throughout the period of human historical record apparently with little change to the present day. In spite of its having millions of speakers around the world, there is little dialect variation among native speakers of Cat, and a grasp of Cat as presented in this book will allow you to converse with Cats of most "breeds"[2] or nations in most areas of the world.

Cat, as has already been discovered by many, is difficult from the beginning. Not only is the tonal element strange to most speakers of Western languages, but in addition the grammar is inseparable from a unique worldview that will challenge many favorite concepts of speakers of human languages. But there is a solution: the more openminded the student is, the more quickly he or she will proceed. It is no good taking offense at the imagined prejudices of Cat grammar. It will be far better for students to examine their own prejudices.

A word about the presentation: the "grammar method" style of teaching a language is out of fashion at the moment,

---

[1] The word "Cat" will be capitalized throughout the text of this book, in defiance of normal English grammatical rules. My advisers point out that the English "cat" is not adequate to express the real nature and meaning of the concept, but it was thought that the use of "HM Cat," although more accurate, would only confuse the reader.

[2] This term is offensive to Cats.

and, indeed, many English speakers have never learned the grammar even of their own language; but in Cat there are important reasons for the methodical presentation of the structure and rules of the language. The language is sacred to Cats, and errors in its use are not tolerated. Grammar mistakes are a particularly dangerous pitfall that must at all costs be avoided; and unless the Cat worldview's effect on the grammar is clearly explained, the student, as well as becoming thoroughly confused, runs the risk of offending Cats, with perhaps profound effects on any subsequent learning. The student must be, and is in the following pages, warned of risky ground. Thus no apology is offered for presenting the language in what some may see as an out-moded format.

THE PRESENTATION

Each chapter in Part One is constructed in the same format. A short passage presenting a simple, everyday situation is followed by a vocabulary list and discussion of the various grammar points raised in the passage, including an explanation of the cultural concepts that may underpin them. Practical spoken and written exercises are then presented.

Part Two must be studied in conjunction with Part One. Here you will learn that Cat is a tonal language—in fact, the most highly tonal of all mammalian languages, and perhaps of all languages of sound. A musical ear is a distinct advantage. The very musical, and especially the violinists among the human population, will find the task of learning Cat significantly easier than the general population.[3] Part Two, then, briefly explains the nature of tonality, and the specific form it takes in Cat. It discusses and explains the Seven Tonal Shapes and the Six Begin Notes, and briefly mentions their role in meaning. Although it is placed second in the text, **Part Two must be thoroughly absorbed before Part One can be put into use, and before any attempt is made to speak the language to a Cat.**

Self-taught students will find the area of tonality daunting at first, especially in the absence of a native speaker. Do not be discouraged: with a little determination, and the use of the charts and a musical instrument such as a violin, it is quite possible for ordinary human beings to learn enough Cat to communiCate with their resident Cats.

A word of warning must go along with any handbook or course of instruction in Cat: *be wary of believing what you are told by even the most beloved of Cats.* The attitude of Cats to what we call "lying" is little understood by humans, who must learn to resist applying human standards to the matter. That there is no word for *truth* in Cat is already well known; what is less generally known, and the impliCations

---

[3] The tone deaf, on the other hand, will be entirely unable to learn Cat, and should make no attempt to speak it at any time. The risk of offending a Cat through error is so high it may be called a certainty.

little appreciated, is that there is also no word for *lie*. Unless, of course (and this must always be borne in mind), Cats are lying to us in this matter.

Cats, it now appears, simply say anything they like. The layperson should bear this fact in mind in every communi-Cation with a Cat. It is extremely unlikely, for example, that any ordinary "house"[4] Cat would have access to information on a conspiracy of Cats to take over the world, even if such a conspiracy existed. The wise will think carefully before calling the Mounties or the CIA with any such information a Cat may impart. And before you go off to Land's End to dig at the foot of a linden tree, pause to ask yourself how "your" Cat knows where the Inca treasure was hidden.

In short, you should be cautious about acting on information received from a Cat, unless such information concerns the Cat's personal wishes or needs. You will learn later in this book how to detect, and the proper ways to respond to, what is called the Fantasy element in Cat.

But even if you do get sent off on one or two embarrassing adventures before this lesson sinks in, you are certain to find the study of Cat exciting and rewarding. My admiration goes out to all those dediCated enough to undertake this exacting study on their own, and I wish you every success in learning how to speak Cat.

---

4   This term is offensive to Cats.

Key to Pronunciation

THE ALPHABET

Cat as a language is not best suited to being transcribed in the Roman alphabet, and indeed, for scholarly purposes an entirely new alphabet has been developed. But for the purposes of self-teaching, it was thought that the disadvantages of the Roman alphabet would be more than offset by the ease of reading; and so an attempt has been made to cast the sounds of Cat into the Roman alphabet—as closely as possible to the sounds represented by those letters in English. Three sounds with no reasonable equivalent in English writing are represented by other marks.

Some of the differences between sounds in Cat—particularly all the sounds clumped under the letter r by the English speaker—are often indetectable to the human ear at first, and this may lead you to make some rather startling errors when you begin (see Chapter Nine, Apology). However, as you listen more closely to native speakers, your ear will soon begin to detect the subtle but very real differences in sound. It may take much longer before you are able to reproduce them accurately, but you will often be comprehensible even through such errors, much as Japanese speakers of English are comprehensible to English native speakers in spite of their r and l confusion.

THE CONSONANTS

There are fifteen consonants in Cat. In written form in this book they are represented as follows:

b – as in "brow" but much less stressed

f – as in "fuss" but with the teeth placed lightly **behind** the lower lip, and not on top of it

h – as in "huh," a short sigh

m – lighter than the English sound—the lips are together but are opened as the sound begins, so there is no "hum"

n – as for **m**, a very light sound

p – as in "praise"; see **b**

r – simple English untrilled **r**, as in "brawl"

rr – trilled **r**. The nearest human equivalent of this sound is formed when the tongue flutters on the hard palate.[1]

R – uvular **r**, as in French "treśor"

RR – heavily rolled uvular **r**

t – as with **b** and **p**

w – the sound made between the **h** and **a** in English "ohh ahh"

^ – glottal breath

` – glottal stop

---

[1] Note that the notation of three or more r's (in Fourth Level Offense and above) indiCates an elongated *untrilled* palatal r.

THE VOWELS

a   –   as in English "flap"

aa –   elongated a, as when humans imitate sheep ("baa")

e   –   as in "left"

ee –   long, as in "peep"

i   –   as in "blip" before a consonant; palatalized before a vowel

o   –   between "box" and "roll," short

u   –   as in "cup," but very short

aw –   as in "oh"

ow –   as in "down," never as in "furrow"

ew –   as in "ewe"

'   –   soft or "breathed" glottal

NOTES ON PRONUNCIATION

1. Vowels that follow r and rr are generally nasalized.

2. As in English, the sound represented by English "w" and "oo" is sometimes a consonant and sometimes a vowel. As a consonant it is an unstressed sound, unless it appears after the diphthong "ow," when it acquires the force of dupliCation, as in meiowwap, "to be hungry."

3. p, t, and m are never exploded when they appear at the end of a word. The sound stops as the lips come together, as if it were swallowed.

4. m is usually palatalized before a vowel—that is, it is followed by a short "y" (as in "you") sound—but there is no firm rule about this, and it varies between speakers.

Never insert a vowel sound between **m** and **a** follow-ing a consonant, however.

5. **n** as with **m**

6. **ow** is pronounced from a very open-mouth position, sliding quickly down to the closed position

7. There is an overall nasality to almost all Cat utter-ances, which is impossible to indiCate in the Roman alphabet, but which is not difficult for human speak-ers to produce. Though North Americans, generally speaking, should make no attempt to increase their own naturally occurring nasality, other English speak-ers can attain this effect by "talking through the nose."

List of Abbreviations

PART ONE

Grammar

Chapter 1

THE PERSONAL PRONOUNS

◆

CAT AND NON-CAT

◆

ADJECTIVES

◆

ADJECTIVAL STRINGS

◆

THE VERB "TO BE" AND CLASS ONE VERBS

◆

SOME RELEVANT NOTES ON ETIQUETTE

mow[1]　　　　　　　The Cat

mow[2] **'aow row mew.**　　The little Cat is cold.

ma`row 'Rowow pwah row.　The pretty coat is wet.

uh rrow uh rowb pwah row.　The whiskers and tail are wet.

mow 'RRaow row.　　The Cat is lonely.

mow merowwap.　　She is hungry.

VOCABULARY

'aow(b1)[3]	little, small	**mRaow**(b3)	food
'Rowow(d2)	pretty, beautiful	**pwah**(c7)	wet
'RRaow(a2)	lonely	**row**(a1, f7)	to be
ma`row(b3)	coat/fur	**rowb**(b6)	tail
merowwap (a1, f7)[4]	to be hungry	**rrow**(b4)	whiskers
mew(c7)	cold	**uh**(a7)	and, also
mow(a1)	Cat, Cat Presence, Higher Being		

[1] This is a lullaby that mother Cats sing to their young.

[2] Capitals are not used to mark the beginning of sentences because of the potential for confusion between **R** and **r**.

[3] The letter and number in brackets refer to the pronunciation code, called the Begin Note—Tonal Shape (BNTS) Code. See Part Two.

[4] The first BNTS refers to Cats; the second to non-Cats.

1 THE PERSONAL PRONOUNS

There are two sets of personal pronouns, those for use by Cats and those for "non-Cats." Humans fall into the latter Category.

Cat

I/we	**mow** (a1)		
you (Cat)	**mowuh** (a4)	*you* (non-Cat)	**ma`**(f7)
she/he/they (C)	**mow** (a1)	*she/he/it/they* (nC)	**ma`**(f7)

Non-Cat

I/we	**ma`**(f7)		
you (nC)	—	*you* (C)	**mow** (a1)
she/he/it (nC)	**ma`**(f7)	*she/he* (C)	**mow** (a1)[5]
they (nC)	**ma`**(f7)	*they* (C)	**mow** (a1)

NOTES ON THE PRONOUNS

a. You will have noticed that there are only three forms — **mow, mowuh** and **ma`**—to serve the seven English pronouns **I, you, she, he, it, we, they.** There is no such thing as a pronoun in Cat. The word **mow**(a1) literally means "Cat Presence/Higher Being." Thus it serves as **I/we** when a Cat is speaking, and **you** when a Cat is being addressed. Although, as mentioned in the section on tonality, Begin Note A carries overtones of plurality, **mow,** Cat Presence, nevertheless exists only in the singular. The much-reported

---

[5] Rare. See under Notes.

idea that "all Cats use the royal We all the time"[6] is, therefore, utter nonsense.

b. There is no distinction between the first person Cat (I/we) and the third person (she, he, they). Cats rarely speak to humans of other Cats; when they do they will use **mow**(a1) and the Cat's "particular"[7] name.

c. ma`, on the other hand, means simply, "non-Cat." Thus a Cat may use it for **you** as well as for **she, he, it, they** when speaking to or of non-Cats. In your own speech, this form means both **I/we** and, when you are speaking of another non-Cat, **she, he, it, they.**

d. You will find these points simple to grasp if you learn to think in Cat terms (Cat Presence, also Cat Presence, non-Cat) rather than in pronouns. The Cat grammatical worldview is not very different in this regard from the widespread human tendency to divide the world grammatically into masculine, feminine, and neuter.

e. You may perhaps hear the third person non-Cat, **ma`**, used by Cats as the "you" form to other Cats. *Never,* under any circumstances, be tempted to use it in this way yourself,

---

[6.] Primarily Dogfodder, "The nature of the A note and the conscious royal prerogative of Cats expressed by the A note–F note split with particular regard to the use among Cats of the pseudo-pronoun **mow** to designate the self," *JCAT,* Vol.3, No. iv, pp. 252–85. He overlooks the distinction between tonal pattern 1 and tonal pattern 4. Furthermore, plurality elsewhere in Cat is clearly considered a negative phenomenon. The use of a plural by Cats would therefore be taken as a sign of humility, not arrogance. But the fact is that **mow** (a1) is not a plural, and therefore bears no relation to the royal We in English. Thus the whole argument falls to the ground.

[7.] For an account of the levels of Cat names, see Eliot, "The Naming of Cats" in *Possum,* p. 1.

even in error. It does not mean "you" or "they" here; in this form it is an insult and must be left to Cats to use among themselves.

    f. Note that there is no second person form for non-Cats to use to non-Cats. *It is an offense for humans to speak to one another in Cat.*[8] (See Chapter Nine, Apology.) Use English or another language. As Cats say, "Dog is good enough."

2 CAT AND NON-CAT

Cat is a language that uses different levels of speech. You have already met the only two levels you will have to learn, Cat and non-Cat.[9] These levels are of the highest importance from the very beginning, because *you may not simply repeat what a Cat says when you are learning a phrase.*

    For example, **mow**(a1) **merowwap**(a1), when spoken by a Cat, translates colloquially, "I'm hungry!" Its literal meaning, however, is "the Cat Presence hungers." The same phrase, when spoken by you, would mean, "You are hungry," and may only be used to address a Cat. It would be considered impertinent of you to inform a Cat of your own hunger, but should you do so, you would say **ma`**(f 7) **merowwap**(f 7),

---

[8] It has become acceptable in classroom situations, but note that in all such human-to-human exchanges, one human must speak as a Cat.

[9] There are other levels of Cat, but these all exist as sub-levels within the Cat level—that is, they are solely for Cats conversing with other Cats—and are of no importance to ordinary human students of the language. They involve a much wider variety of Tonal Shapes and Begin Notes than you will study in this book, and are extremely difficult for humans. Much of such communiCation apparently involves insult.

literally, "non-Cat hungers." This phrase would be virtually meaningless to a Cat, as it would appear to be a peculiarly uninteresting statement about the general nature of non-Cat.

The two levels of the language will henceforward be signaled by C and nC in this textbook. The same two divisions will refer to the speakers. The context should make clear which is meant. In the following chart:

C

leave me alone (nC)! − **maaa`(f 7)**

maaa` is the form for a Cat addressing a non-Cat. Thus the **C** indiCates that the form is for **use by Cats**, and the (nC) that it is the form for **addressing non-Cats.**

NOTE: The popular idea that these different levels of speech in Cat involve status is mistaken. No judgment whatsoever is implied by the distinction between Cat and non-Cat. The distinction is entirely *grammatical.*

3 ADJECTIVES

An adjective modifies a noun. That is to say, it is a word used to describe some person, place, thing, or idea. In the phrase, "Dogfodder's ideas are unsound," *unsound* is an adjective[10] modifying the noun *ideas.*

[10.] Specifically, of course, a subjective completion of the copula verb.

Adjectives may precede or follow the noun they modify, or both. They may also stand alone.

'aow mow – little Cat
rowb 'Rowow – pretty tail

4 ADJECTIVAL STRINGS

When two or more adjectives are used in conjunction, they are joined by **uh**—"and."

mew uh 'RRaow uh 'aow mow – cold, lonely, little Cat

A noun may also be bracketed by adjectives. In this case **uh** is not needed, as the noun takes its place.

'Rowow mow 'aow – beautiful little Cat

5 THE VERB "TO BE"

	C		nC	
I am/we are	**mow**(a1) **row**(a1)		**ma`**(f 7) **row**(f 7)	
you (C) are	**mowuh**(a4) **row**(a1)		**mow**(a1) **row**(a1)	
you (nC) are	**ma`**(f 7) **row**(f 7)		–	
she/he/they (C) are	**mow**(a1) **row**(a1)		**mow**(a1) **row**(a1)	
she/he/it (nC)	**ma`**(f 7) **row**(f 7)		**ma`**(f 7) **row**(f 7)	
they (nC) are	**ma`**(f 7) **row**(f 7)		**ma`**(f 7) **row**(f 7)	

CLASS ONE VERBS

a. Verbs indiCating state of being rather than action are called Class One verbs. They follow the pattern of the verb **row**: Cat verbs take the BNTS **a1** and non-Cat verbs the BNTS **f7**.

mow merowwap(a1) – you(C) are hungry

b. All inanimate objects and nonsentient nature take the Cat form of the verb.

mRaow mew(c7) **row**(a1) – the food is cold

6 WRITTEN EXERCISE

Find the words for the following (choose the non-Cat level of speech):

    1 Cat.
    2 You (C) are pretty.
    3 The little Cat is hungry.
    4 You (C) are cold and wet.
    5 Food.

7 COMPREHENSION EXERCISE[11]

mow(a1). **mow**(a1) **'Rowow**(d2) **row**(a1). **mow**(a1) **merowwap**(a1). **mRaow**(b3) **mew**(c7) **row**(a1). **rrow**(b4) **row**(a1) **pwah**(c7).

8 PRACTICAL EXERCISES WITH A NATIVE
SPEAKER[12]

For your first session, use ordinary methods of gaining the Cat's attention: a bit of cheese or a deliCate scratching motion on whatever part of the anatomy the Cat presents. Adopt a relaxed posture.

If the Cat pays no attention, *do not make a kissing or sucking noise.* This generally gains the Cat's negative attention, and will be counterproductive. Simply abandon your efforts and try another time.

When you have the Cat's attention, quietly repeat the expression **ma`**, on Begin Note F and Tonal Shape 7. This indiCates your willingness to be of service. *Your attitude should above all be humble.*

Do not expect a response at once. The Cat may need time to overcome its surprise. Say the word two or three times and then return to ordinary human/Cat communiCation. The Cat will now find ways to indiCate what service might be acceptable at this time. Be sure to oblige.

[11.] For a translation of this and subsequent exercises, see Appendix B.

[12.] To be omitted by those without access to a native speaker.

Chapter 2

"MUST" AND OTHER DEFECTIVE VERBS

♦

FORMS OF GREETING

♦

THE NEGATIVE

♦

THE ADJECTIVAL BREATH

♦

ADVERBS

♦

INTENSIFIERS

♦

THE VERB "TO HAVE" AND CLASS TWO VERBS

SCENE:

A human meets the neighbor's Cat in the garden.
The following conversation ensues.

CAT: **mow**(a1).	How do you do?
HUMAN: **mow. ma`(f 7).**	How do you do, Honored Cat? I am at liberty at the moment. Can I be of service?
CAT: **ma` mupRup**(f 7) **birr**(b5) **birr pirp**(c4)	A dish of cream, if you would be so kind.
HUMAN: **birr birr ma` bra!**	Cream coming up!

The human brings a dish of cream and offers it.
The Cat drinks the cream.

CAT: **mbruuh**(a5)	Thank you!
HUMAN: **ma` RRow**(a1). **ma`?**	My pleasure, certainly. Is there anything else?

The Cat leaves.

VOCABULARY

birr(b5)	milk	**mbruuh**	thank you
birr(b5)**birr**[1]	cream	(a5)(C)	
bra(c4)(nC)	to work; lift,	**mi'ao**(a4)	garden
	carry, fetch; do	**nmbruh**(f 7)	unpleasant
ma`RRow	thank you	**pirp**(c4)(nC)	to bring; offer,
(a1)(nC)			make an offering to
mbruh(b5)	nice, pleasant	**ruh**(b4, c4)	to intend, mean
mbruuh(a5)	pleased		

1 THE VERB "MUST"

C

you (nC) *must*	– mupRup(f 7)[2]
she/he/it/they (nC) *must*	– mupRup

nC

I/we must	– mupRup
it/they (nC) *must*	– mupRup

a. mupRup is a defective verb. There is no form of **mupRup** to use to a Cat. Never use any form of this verb to give a Cat an order. It is a grammatical error of the gravest nature. (See Chapter Nine, Apology.)

---

[1] Note the section on intensifiers below.
[2] Note that, as a Class One verb, *must* is considered a state of being. Cats do not experience such a state of being. Thus the verb is defective.

b. mupRup is followed by the verb in its normal conjugated form.

mupRup bra(c4) – please do it![3]

DEFECTIVE VERBS

There are certain verbs which, like **mupRup**, exist only in
the non-Cat form. Class One defective verbs follow the
mupRup pattern. In this book they are notated (f 7)(nC).

2 FORMS OF GREETING

As you have learned in Chapter One, **mow**(a1), the word
used by Cats as the first person pronoun (I/we), means
"Cat Presence." This word is also the most common Cat
greeting, generally used by Cats upon entering a room. The
word may never be used in this way by a human, since the
substance of it is to announce the arrival of Cat Presence. It
may be used in response to a Cat greeting, then signifying,
"I acknowledge Cat Presence."

You may find yourself in a situation where you wish to
greet a Cat who has not previously greeted you. Generally
speaking, this is a social solecism unless the Cat addressed is
hungry.[4] However, the rules here, as elsewhere, are looser

---

[3] Lit. "you (nC) must do it," but in this and similar contexts the Cat should not be seen
as giving an order, but merely commenting, as it were, on the state of being of the
human. "I know that your (good) nature compels you" is closer to the state of mind of
a Cat using this verb.

[4] But see Eliot, "The Ad-dressing of Cats," for an alternate view: "Myself, I do not hold
with that. I say, you should ad-dress a Cat." *Possum*, p. 54f.

than they used to be. In such circumstances, to avoid giving offense, it is best to say **ma`(f 7)**, "non-Cat." In this context the word signifies "servant" and implies a readiness to engage in some duty that will be pleasing to the Cat.

The most polite (and welcome) form of address is the well-known **mRaow(b3)**,[5] but students are reminded that this word means literally "food," and should only be used when it is to be followed by a real offer of food.

3 THE NEGATIVE

a. The negative is formed by adding the sound **n** before the part of speech to be negatived. English speakers use the sound whenever they shorten the word "and," as in the phrase "It's raining Cats 'n' dogs."[6] In Cat, the sound is shorter. There is no BNTS for **n** because its Tonal Shape consists entirely of its Begin Note, which it takes from the word it precedes.

nmow(a1) – non-Cat[7]

The negative may be attached to any part of speech. **mRaow nrow** and **nmRaow row** both signify, "It's inedible."

---

[5] See Chapter Four for another acceptable greeting.

[6] This phrase is deeply offensive to Cats. It is used here through necessity. See Chapter Nine, Apology.

[7] This word is not in general use among Cats. Most Cats feel that the word **mow(a1)** is sacred, and cannot be used in any way in reference to a non-Cat. Some Cats may use it to a favored human as a sign of particular benevolence. It is given here as a grammatical example only. The accepted form for non-Cat is given above: **ma`(f 7)**.

b. Negative turns of phrase figure prominently in the speech of non-Cats, and you should be sure to learn it. It is particularly useful for apology, as in:

ma`(f 7) nruh(f 7) – I didn't mean it

4 THE ADJECTIVAL BREATH

a. Adjectives carry a "non-Cat" signifier when they are used to describe a sentient being other than a Cat. This is an almost silent breath added to the end of the adjective. It is indiCated by the sign ^.

mbruh^ ma` – nice human

b. This sound also appears on its own, when it indiCates a high degree of positive interest in a non-Cat – ^^. In this rarely used form, delivered with the mouth wide open, it has become popularly known as "the silent miaow", although it is more properly called the glottal squeak. It is generally used to disarm humans.[8]

  c. The adjectival breath is difficult for most humans to pronounce, but it is seldom necessary because of the indifference Cats feel toward any discussion of non-Cats. Remember that Cats have a great deal on their minds. Keep your use of non-Cat adjectives to a minimum.

---

[8] The open-mouthed hiss ^^^^^^ is etymologically related; it indiCates high degree of negative interest in anything.

ma` 'aow^ row(f 7) – she (nC) is small[9]

NOTE: Inanimate objects and non-sentient nature[10] do not require the adjectival breath.

birr mew row(a1) – the milk is cold

5 ADVERBS

There is no distinction between adjectives and adverbs.

mow mieh(d1) **row** – the Cat is dainty
mow mieh(d1) **rro** – the Cat washes daintily

6 INTENSIFIERS

There is no universal intensifier in Cat equivalent to the English "very." An adjective or adverb is intensified in two ways, doubling and bracketing.

'Rowow(d2) **'Rowow mow**(a1) – very pretty cat
(lit. pretty pretty Cat)

---

[9] **mah**(f 7), "Really" (NA) or "Quite" (Eng) or is often the response to this sort of unnecessary statement, if a Cat hears it at all. While the word expresses a minimal degree of interest, is cannot be translated, as Dogfodder suggests, by "ho hum."

[10] Rechter suggests that mice, birds, and other *edible* sentient creatures do not take the adjectival breath. This would only be in a case where a Cat was visualizing the bird as already nonsentient, however. It is akin to omitting the use of the future tense where intent is high, as in the French *j'arrive!*

or

'Rowow mow 'Rowow   – (lit. pretty Cat pretty)
mow mowruh(b4) arp(b4)   – she runs incredibly fast
    mowruh

7 THE VERB "TO HAVE"

	C	nC
I/we have	mow(a1) row(b4)	ma`(f 7) row(c4)\
you (C) *have*	mowuh(a4) row(b4)	mow(a1) row(b4)
you (nC) *have*	ma`(f 7) row(c4)	—
she/he (C) *has*	mow(a1) row(b4)	mow(a1) row(b4)
they (C) *have*	mow(a1) row(b4)	mow(a1) row(b4)
she/he/it (nC)	ma`(f 7) row(c4)	ma`(f 7) row(c4)
they (nC) *have*	ma`(f 7) row(c4)	ma`(f 7) row(c4)

Note that the consonant–vowel cluster is the same as for the verb "to be," **row**. But here there is a different Begin Note and Tonal Shape, and therefore there is no confusion in meaning.

CLASS TWO VERBS

All action verbs follow the pattern of the verb **row**(b4), to have. They are called Class Two verbs. Cat verbs take the BNTS b4 and non-Cat verbs the BNTS c4.

CLASS TWO DEFECTIVE VERBS

As with Class One verbs, certain Class Two verbs exist only in the non-Cat form. These describe action performed exclusively by non-Cats. They are notated (c4)(nC).

ma` bra(c4) **birr** – I (nC) am fetching milk

8 COMPREHENSION EXERCISE

birr row(a1) **mbruh. pwah ma`row mbruh nrow**(a1). **mow 'aow row**(b4) **rowb 'aow. mupRup birr pirp.**

9 PRACTICAL EXERCISES WITH A NATIVE SPEAKER

Choose a moment when the Cat is in the kitchen.[11] Stand by the refrigerator or a cupboard where food is stored. Say **mRaow**(b3) quietly once or twice. Carefully note the Cat's response. If she says **birr**(b5) or **birr birr**, respond with the appropriate food. If you cannot clearly understand the response, any tidbit or snack of which the Cat is particularly fond may now be offered.

Practice this exercise as often as you wish.

---

[11] This is best done when it is *not* the Cat's regular mealtime.

Chapter 3

POSSESSIVES

◆

THE NEGATIVE POSSESSIVE

◆

THE PAST TENSE

◆

GOD

◆

FOOD

◆

PERFECT VERBS

bRRow(d1) uh(a7) 'aa(d1)[1]

bRRow(d1) berah(a1) bRRow(b4). mew(d4) bRRow(d1) mRRow(b4). 'aa(d1) mrow(b4) bRRow(d1) ruh(a7) mRRaow(a3)[2] 'aa(c7) Row(a4) maow(b4).

mew(a4) 'aa miaow(b4): *mew*(d4) *mow*(a1) *pra*(b7) *mraow*(b4) *uh*(a7) *irr*(a5) *mRRah*(a4) *row*(b4). *m'mow*(a1) *row*(a1). *mowuh*(a4) *pra*(a7) *nmow*(b4) *m'mow mRRah*(a4).[3]

bRRow(d1) mow(b4) m' 'aa(d1) mRRah(a4). 'aa(d1) bRRow(a1).

'aa(d1) miaow(b4): *mow*(a1) *pra*(c7) *bRRow*(b4)!

bRRow(d1) rro(b4) rowb(b6). bRRow(d1) broh(b4) mRRaow(a3) nrow(b4), broh(b4) 'aa pra(c7) bRRow(b4).

bRRow(d1) bRRow(a1).

bRRow(d1) miaow(b4): *bRRow*(a6) *mbruh*(b5) *row. mow*(a1) *uh*(a7) *ar*(a1) *bRRow*(b4) *ruh*(a7) *m' 'aa bRRow*(a6)!

---

[1] For a version of this story in English, see Appendix A.

[2] "BRRow's testicles." Parts of the body are not signified through the possessive. See Chapter Five, Attributes.

[3] "Do not eat my tidbits" (lit. "You have not eaten my titbits"). This use of the past as an imperative is for Cat-to-Cat communiCation *only,* and would be ungrammatical if used by a human. See Chapter Five, Imperatives.

VOCABULARY

'a(a7)	if	miew(a2, a4)	tuna/flesh
'aa(d1)	'Aa (name)	mow(b4)(C)	to eat
'aa(c7)	on, in	mraow(b4, c4)	to hunt
berah(a1, f7)	to like	maowr(a2, a4)	salmon/flesh
broh(b4, c4)	to see	mRRah(a4)	tidbit, snack
broh(a4)	eye	mRRaow(a3)	testicles
bRRow(a1,f7)	to laugh[3]	mRRow	to sleep, com-
bRRow(a6)	joke, trick	(b4)(C)	mune with Mow[4]
bRRow(b4)(C)	to play tricks	pra(c7)	already, before,
bRRow(d1)	BRRow the		yesterday, "the
	trickster		time before"
maow(b4, c4)	to place, put	prrew(a2, a4)	mouse/meat
mrow(b4)(C)	to take	pwah(f7)	water
mew(a4)	(in the) morning	Row(a4)	bowl, dish
mew(d4)	night, at night	rro(b4, c4)	to wash, clean
miaow(b4)(C)	to talk, say	ruh(a7)	like, similar to

1 POSSESSIVES

a. The Possessive Particle

Possession is indiCated by the addition of the particle **m'** to the possessor. The thing possessed follows[5] the possessor. The particle **m'** adopts the Begin Note of the word it modifies.

---

[3] Note that "to laugh" is a state of being, not an action.

[4] "To sleep" is a Class Two perfect verb. This is not an exception to the rule. Sleep performed by Cats is considered active.

[5] Sometimes, for considerations of style, the possessed object may precede the possessor, but this is not usual in ordinary conversation.

m'mow(a1) **Row**(a4) – the Cat's dish
m' 'aa(d1) **bRRow**(a6) – 'Aa's joke

The possessive particle may be attached only to the nouns **mow** and **mowuh** or to a Cat's name. *It is never used to indiCate possession by a non-Cat.*

b. Possession by non-Cat—the Negative Possessive
Although in practice many Cats do recognize ownership by humans, grammatically there is no precise way to indiCate that a non-Cat owns anything. Non-Cat possession is implied in the negative possessive "not belonging to Cat."[6] There are good historical reasons for this, which have little to do with popular notions of "Cats feeling they own the world." Cats do not feel any such thing. Remember the proverb, **'a m'mow**(a1) **row, m'mow**(d4) **row; 'a m'mow**(a1) **nrow, m'mow**(d4) **row**—"If it is mine, it is God's; if it is not mine, it is God's."[7]

Generally speaking, you will not need to indiCate particular non-Cat ownership to a Cat. Remember that Cats are

---

[6] Another (very recent) form, **m'ma`**, with the literal meaning, "belonging to non-Cat," has been noted, but this is a neologism, which only the most liberal of Cats is likely to use. Do not expect it even from a Cat who is very fond of you. No related form **m'ma`** exists for use by non-Cats. It would be an offense for you to indiCate positive ownership of anything. (See Chapter Nine, Apology.)

[7] Elsewhere mistranslated as, "If it is mine, it is mine; if it is not mine, it is mine." See Dogfodder, "Mine, mine and not-yours: problems with the possessive" in *JCAT,* Vol 9, No. i, pp. 11–19. Dogfodder's attested tone-deafness is a barrier to his comprehension of Cat speech, never more grotesquely apparent than here, where he completely misses the distinction between a1 and d4!

not very interested in such details. Where you are absolutely certain that such information is essential to a Cat, there are other ways than the grammatical possessive to indiCate it.

mRaow(b3) m'mow – the food is not yours; it is Blacky's
   nrow Blacky   (lit. the food is not yours—
                             Blacky)[8]

Here the statement of non ownership by the Cat is fol lowed by the name of the actual owner.[9]

c. The Possessive Pronoun Adjectives[10]

C

my, mine	m'mow(a1)		
your, yours (C)	m'mowuh(a4)	*your/s* (nC)	nm'mow(a1)[11]
their, theirs (C)	m'mow(a1)	*its, theirs* (nC)	nm'mow(a1)

nC

my, mine	nm'mow(a1)	*your, yours* (C)	m'mow(a1)
its, theirs (nC)	nm'mow(a1)	*their, theirs* (C)	m'mow(a1)

---

[8] Here, of course, Blacky is not a Cat. Where Blacky is a Cat the form will be **mRaow m'mow Blacky row**—"the food is Blacky's."

[9] It should be noted that most Cats would consider the addition of the name redundant, and possibly insulting. (See Chapter Nine, Apology.) That the food is not for the Cat is sufficiently unwelcome information. The notion that food *by right* belongs to someone else is grammatically so ridiculous as to be almost incomprehensible.

[10] Strictly speaking, these are neither pronouns nor adjectives, but rather nouns with the possessive particle attached. But the chart may be of use to nonnative speakers.

[11] Literally, "not belonging to Cat."

m'mow mRRah(a4) – your (C) tidbits (also "Cat's tidbits")
m'mow mRRah   – my (C) tidbits

The possessive pronoun is not always used. Where possession is understood, it may be omitted.

bRRow rro mRRaow – BRRow cleaned (his) sexual parts.[12]

2 THE PAST TENSE

Cats are rarely concerned about any time other than the
present. What humans call the past tense[13] is indiCated by
putting the past particle **pra**(c7), "already, before, yesterday,
the time before," before the verb.

bRRow mRRaow(a3) **pra brap**(b4) – BRRow ate his
                                              testicles

Where it is not required for sense, it may be omitted.

mow mRRah(a4) **brap** – the Cat ate the tidbits (the
                                  Cat is eating the tidbits)

3 GOD

To Cats, God is a Cat. This fact is an intrinsic part of the language, and the concept is an important one to any student of

---

[12] This in any case is not a possessive relationship, but an attribute. See Chapter Five.
[13] Human perception of time is defective.

Cat. The word for God, **mow**(d4),[14] will be seen to have the same consonant–vowel cluster as the word for Cat and the first-person pronoun, with a different Begin Note and Tonal Shape. As you will see in the section on Begin Notes, the D Begin Note (BN D) implies particular femaleness, that is, over and above what might be called the general femaleness of everything.

BN D further carries the impliCation of unity, oneness, while BN A implies diversity. This curious (to humans) reference to the "personal I" Cat Presence as diversity, and the "overall" Cat Presence as unity is hard for us, but not apparently for Cats, to comprehend on a metaphysical or philosophical level. It is made more complex by the fact that, as will be explained in the section on Tonality, BN D also implies and includes BN A (and not vice versa).

Thus it will be seen that the word **mow**(d4) carries a multitude of virtually untranslatable connotations, which might in English be incompletely expressed as "I All and One (the Divine Great She) Cat Presence."

MOW AND HUMANS

The understood "I" component of the word **mow** makes the use of the word a difficult area for humans. There are Cat freethinkers who accept that the "All and One" component of Godhead includes all sentient beings as well as nonsentient

---

[14] Literally, of course, "Goddess."

nature (which is included as a matter of course). Such free-thinkers point out that although the word arose at a time and place where no sentient species other than Cat existed, it was meant as a universal concept. Thus, they say, even humans have the right to express themselves as part of divinity.

Cat purists, however—and they are in the majority—point out that the third-person pronoun **ma`(f 7)** implies a level of diversity approaching chaos, and therefore non-Cats do not partake of the divinity shared by Cats. A Cat holding this belief will be deeply offended by any attempt on your part to discuss Mow, because you by your nature are incapable of using the word.[15] You are advised to be very, very sure that a Cat is a freethinker before undertaking any such discussion, and indeed, you ought not to attempt anything of this nature until you are far more fluent in Cat than this book can make you. (See Chapter Nine, Apology.)

4 FOOD

Much as English makes a distinction between *cow* and *beef,* Cat always makes a distinction between potential food, which is still living, and the meat obtained from it. Thus **maowr**(a4), "salmon," indiCates that which comes out of a tin, while **maowr**(a2) refers to the living fish.

---

[15] Yet it is clear that ancient peoples—the Sumerians, for example—were encouraged to worship Mow. Bright, in "Is collective Cat memory long enough?," *UBCAT*, Vol. V, No. 1, pp. 13–46, argues that the prejudice against human use of the word **mow**(d4) is a very late development.

As you learned in Chapter One, all nonsentient nature, and therefore inert forms of food, take the Cat form of the verb. This is partly because the closer something is to being eaten by a Cat, the closer it is to absorption in Godhead. A second and more significant reason is that food is generally sccn as an offering to Mow, and takes on virtue.

Food that is still living, of course, takes the non-Cat form of the verb.

maowr(a4) **'aa Row**(a4) **row**(a1)   – the salmon (flesh) is
                                                                        in the bowl
maowr(a2) **'aa pwah**(f 7) **row**(f 7) – the (living) salmon
                                                                        is in the water

5 PERFECT VERBS

Just as some verbs (defective verbs, Chapter Two) can be conjugated only in the non-Cat form, so there are certain verbs that can be conjugated only in the Cat form. These are called perfect verbs. They indiCate actions or states of being that only Cats experience. They follow the Cat form of Class One and Two verbs.

prip(b4)   – grant, bestow, dispense, give,
                                         vouchsafe
mow prip(b4) **ma`** – you may bring food (lit. "I grant
  mRaow pirp(c4)   that you may offer food")[16]

---

[16] Note the difference between the perfect verb **prip**(b4)—to bestow, grant or vouchsafe, and the defective verb **pirp**(c4)—to give or offer, make an offering.

These verbs are indiCated in the vocabulary with the notation (C) after the BNTS.

6 COMPREHENSION EXERCISE

m'mow(a1)   mRaow(a3)   'aa(c7)   Row(a4)   row(a1).
maowr(a2) 'aa pwah(f 7) praow(c4). mRaow(b3) mow(a1)
bRuh(b4). mew(d4) mow(a1) pra mraow(b4) uh mew(a4)
mow pra bRRow(b4) uh bRRow(a1).

7 PRACTICE EXERCISES

1. 'Aa played a good joke. BRRow laughed.
2. I (nC) have put the tuna in your (C) bowl.
3. I (nC) have cleaned your bowl.
4. Last night the Cat played a trick and we (nC) laughed.
5. In the morning, the Cat likes to eat a tidbit.

8 TEST FOR PROGRESS

The story of BRRow and 'Aa, presented at the beginning of the chapter, is much loved by Cats. Ask your Cat to listen while you read it to her. Monitor the Cat's response. If she laughs,[17] congratulations! You have been studying well.

---

[17] Remember that the Cat laugh is bRRow(d1)!

The Cat may offer some corrections in your pronunciation. Listen carefully.

If the Cat does not laugh, or if she loses attention and walks away before the story is finished, you are not ready to proceed beyond this chapter. Go over the sections on tonality again.

Chapter 4

THE FLATTERY VOICE

◆

QUESTIONS

◆

ATTRIBUTES

◆

THE PLURAL

◆

DEFINITE AND INDEFINITE

maow(d4)	**Song**[1]
mow 'R<u>o</u>w<u>ow</u>(d2)	you (are) pretty
mow w<u>a</u>h(d1)	you (are) handsome
rrow mb<u>o</u>h	big whiskers
b'row uh b'row b'row(d1)	unnumbered hairs[2]
mbruh ma`r<u>o</u>w(b3)	a fine coat
broh m<u>eo</u>w(d4)	discerning eye
mir m<u>eo</u>w	sharp claw
rowb(b6)	(the parts adjacent to) the tail
rro(d4)	clean
rir(d4)	(you are worthy of) music
mbo(d3)	(you are worthy of the) name
rir	music
mrruh	name
uhmeuh	nine
mow(d4) **mbruuh**(d1)	Mow is pleased (with you)

---

[1] This is a song Cats tend to sing when sitting in bright sunlight, having cleaned themselves after a good meal. In modern times it has become quite permissible for a human to sing the song to a Cat.

[2] Lit. "hairs of" hair. See Chapter Seven.

VOCABULARY

^ow(f4)(nC)	pants, jeans; skin; clothes	m'aaw (b4)(C)	to fight (nobly), to engage in battle
arp(b4, c4)	to run, scurry	meow(d1)	today
b'row(d1)	hair	meow(d4)	good, sharp, clear
b'row uh b'row	"hairs of," i.e., many, numerous, uncountable	mir(d1)	claw, claws
		mrrew(f 7)	name(nC)
brap(b4, c4)	to eat	mrruh(d3)	name (C)
broh(a4)	eye	rir(d4)	music
brroh(d4)	shadow	rowb(b6)	tail
maow(d4)	song	Row^(b1)	lap, knee
maowro (b4, c4)	to sing	rro(d4)	cleanliness
mbruuh (a1, d1)[3]	to be pleased with, to approve	waa` (c4)(nC)	to scrap, to fight
		wah(d1)	handsome

1 THE FLATTERY VOICE

There is no exact equivalent of the Flattery Voice in any European language. This is a form of the verb that denotes a degree of certainty higher than that expressed in the indiCative mood. The indiCative is used in statements of fact, such as, "She is irritated," and the subjunctive in statements of doubt or possibility, such as, "I think that she may

---

[3] See Chapter Seven, Class Three verbs.

be musical." The Flattery Voice might be expressed by the statement, "It is certain that she is offended" or "What a fine voice she has!"

The Flattery Voice is formed by elongating the vowel sound of adjectives. Sometimes the word order may be changed. Verbs of state of being may be omitted.

mow row 'Rowow–   you are beautiful
                                 (indiCative)

mow 'Rowow – you are so beautiful; how beautiful
                           you are!

WHEN TO USE THE FLATTERY VOICE

a. A Cat may indiCate willingness to hear the Flattery Voice in one of three ways:

1. by arching the back invitingly
2. by pressing the head firmly against some part of a human's body
3. by repeating **rrup**(a1)[4] one or several times

However, the Flattery Voice needs no invitation. Many Cats now consider a statement in the Flattery Voice a sufficient introduction from a human, and in such cases, it

---

[4] **rrup** has no English equivalent. It has been called the "Invitation to Intimacy." You should always make a communiCation in the Flattery Voice when you hear this word.

would have the same weight as the more traditional offer of food, **mRaow,** outlined in Chapter Two.[5]

In situations where you have reason to believe that a Cat may be hungry, however, you should retain the traditional form of greeting.[6]

b. A communiCation in the Flattery Voice must always precede and follow any discussion of a Cat other than the one with whom you are speaking. This is called the bracket or parenthesis, and the effect is exactly what that term indiCates: to mark the communiCation as secondary to the main topic (admiration of the Cat).[7]

1. **mow 'Rowow**   –   my, you're looking
    meow   lovely today!
2. **mow Lorna nrow?**   –   Lorna Cat not around?
3. **uh wah ma`row**   –   and you have an extremely
    wah mow row(b4)!   handsome coat!

---

[5] This fact may be explained by the fact that, like humans, Cats tend to be better fed now than in the past, and therefore pleasing descriptions of the Cat are quite as welcome as food.

[6] You may be surprised to hear Cats use the Flattery Voice among themselves in situations where it is clear compliment is not intended. Between equals, the Flattery Voice is called the Descriptive Voice, and may also be used to express disapproval. You should never under any circumstances attempt to use it in this fashion. *Humans should not express, or indeed feel, disapproval of Cats.* It is grammatically unsound. See Chapter Nine, Apology.

[7] The rules for conducting historical discussions are more complex than this, and beyond the scope of this work—and your abilities at this level. Beware!

2 QUESTIONS

Direct questions are rare in Cat; they are considered rude.[8]
Information is elicited in other ways.

a. Statement

A Cat whose dinner is late will not, unless extremely inconvenienced, ask, "Where is my dinner?" Instead,

m'mow m'ow(d1) nrow	– my dinner is not in my
'aa Row	dish
mupRup m'mow m'ow pirp	– you must bring my
	dinner[9]

b. Challenge

Where information rather than action is desired, the
Challenge form—stating something as fact and waiting to

---

[8] Since there is so much misinformation at present about it, a word must be said here about 'arra. This is the "true" question form. The word 'arra(a7), placed immediately before any sentence, takes the place of the English words Who, What, Where, When, Why, depending on the context.

> 'arra row(f 7)?   —   What is it?
> 'arra ma` row?   —   Who are you (nC)?

However, as a number of syntactical louts and fools have discovered, 'arra may also be used as a general term of abuse. Thus, in certain circumstances, the questions above are not so much an expression of interest as a term of opprobrium, perhaps better translated respectively as, "What the bleep is this?" and "Who the devil are you?"

For this reason you should make no attempt to use the true question form until you have attained a high degree of fluency in Cat. Any use of this term to enquire into a Cat's likes, dislikes or activities, for example, would be a grave offense. (See Chapter Nine, Apology.) Use the "challenge" form for questioning.

[9] In extreme cases, this may be spoken in the Offended Voice. See Chapter Seven.

be challenged—is used. Non-Cats may use the Challenge form of question in certain circumstances.

mow merowwap   –   are you hungry? (lit. you
                                       [Cat] are hungry)

The verb **bRuh**(b4) "desire, wish" may be used in the chal-lenge form:

mow bRuh(b4) **birr**(b5)   –   would you (C) like
                                      some milk? (lit. you
                                      would like milk)
mow bRuh ma`birr(b1) **bra**   –   shall I fetch you a
                                      cushion? (you would
                                      like me to fetch a
                                      cushion)

3 ATTRIBUTES

mow ruh(a/) **rrow**   –   the Cat's whiskers

a. It probably struck you, during the discussion of posses-sives in Chapter Three, that without a non-Cat possessive, you have no way to indiCate such things as "the dog's tail," "my (nC) knee," and the like.

Cat does not consider that *attributes* are in a possessed relationship with the creature they define. This is called the "attributive" relationship. The pronoun or noun is followed by the word **ruh** (a7, c7) and then by the attribute.[10]

mow(a1) **maow**(b4)   – are you going to come
  uh prruh(a1) **'aa ma**`(f 7)   and sit on my (nC) lap?
  ruh(c7) **Row^**(b1)   (lit. the Cat Presence is
                              coming and sitting on me
                              as defined by lap)

maaa` **mow**(a1) **ruh**(a7)   – get off my (C) tail!
  rowb!

b. *In extremis,* the attribute construction may be used to indiCate non-Cat possession, but it must be stressed that no Cat will tolerate repeated use of this essentially ungrammatical construct.[11]

---

[10] The opposite construction is also common. **ma**` **ruh Row^** — "me as defined by lap"; **Row^ ruh ma**` — "lap as an attribute of me."

[11] Always think twice before using any non-Cat possessive. Ask yourself if it is really a necessary communiCation *from the Cat's point of view.* In the writer's opinion, the statement here is totally unnecessary. Both you and the Cat know how the hairs got on your trousers. Furthermore, the whole thing fails in its intent (being, of course, to induce guilt in the Cat) since to a Cat the leaving of hairs on anything constitutes a blessing. For this reason the Cat (who does not like to have her generosity drawn attention to, and certainly will not stand being thanked) will ignore the whole communiCation.

b'row uh b'row' b'row   – there are hairs all over my
aa ma` ruh ^ow(a4)   pants. Have you been
row. mow pra prruh 'aa ^ow taking your ease on them?[12]

4 THE PLURAL

a. Plural nouns[13]

1. Two repetitions of a noun indiCate the number two or simply the idea of plurality.

mow pra brap prrew prrew   – I ate (a brace of) mice

2. Two repetitions joined by **uh** ("and") indiCate "many."

mow brap prrew uh prrew   – I eat a lot of mice

3. An undefined plural is served by the singular.

awa(f 7) morh(c4)   – the dog bites, or dogs bite

b. Plural nouns with Class One verbs

1. Two singular subjects, when not mixed, will normally take one verb.

---

[12] Lit. "you have taken your ease on my pants." Remember never to use the **'arra** form of question under any circumstances. **'arra mow prruh 'aa ma` ruh ^ow**, for example, would not translate simply, "Have you been lying on my pants?" but something like, "Have you been defeCating hair all over my bleeping pants, dingbat?" and most Cats would find this offensive. It is doubtful if even a Ninth-Level apology would be effective after such a grammatical solecism. (See Chapter Nine, Apology.)

[13] For nouns defined by numbers, see Chapter Seven, Numbers.

mow uh mow Maureen – are you(C) and Maureen
m`ma` bRRow(a1)   Cat laughing at me?

2. Cat and non-Cat may never be served by the same Class
One verb.[14]

mow bRRow(a1) **uh ma`** – you(C) and I(nC) are
bRRow(f 7)   laughing

c. Plural nouns with Class Two verbs

1. Again, where two singular subjects are unmixed, they
share a verb.

mow uh mow Blacky – Blacky and I would like a
bRuh(b4) **mRRah**   snack

2. Because Class Two verbs indiCate action taken, the non-
Cat form of the verb may be omitted where a Cat verb
already conveys the sense. The non-Cat pronoun does not
precede the Cat verb.

mow arp(b4) **uh prrew** – you (C) and the mouse ar
                                running

---

[14] Because they indiCate state of being. It may be true, as Antichat has pointed out, that
"*il y a deux* niveaux *d'état d'éxistence, et certainement l'état d'éxistence de chat est plus
élevé que celui de non-chat,*" CH, vol. 2 no. i, page 16, but such speculation is unnecessary for the elucidation of what is, after all, a simple point of grammar.

NOTE: The Cat form of the verb may never be omitted. *No Cat subject may ever be served by a non-Cat verb.*

d. Perfect Verbs with Defective Verbs

A defective verb may not be omitted in conjunction with a perfect verb.

mow m'aaw(b4) uh awa(f 7) waa`(c4)	–	the Cat and dog are fighting[15]

e. Plural adjectives

Adjectives do not agree in number with nouns.

mir(d1) mcow	–	sharp claw
mir mir meow	–	sharp claws

The plural noun may bracket the adjective modifier.

mrruh mowruh mrruh	–	noble names

5 DEFINITE AND INDEFINITE

There are no articles equivalent to the English "the" and "a."

mow broh prrew	–	I (C) see *a* mouse
mow broh prrew	–	I (C) see *the* mouse

---

[15] Lit. "the Cat is engaged in noble battle and a dog is scrapping pitifully," but such purely grammatical distinctions should, at this level of study, be ignored.

6 COMPREHENSION EXERCISE

'R<u>owow</u>(d2) mow 'R<u>owow</u> 'R<u>owow</u>. mow broh(a4) meow(d4) row(b4) uh prrew pra broh(b4). prrew ruh rowb irr irr (pra) row(a1)? irr irr row(a1).

7 PRACTICE EXERCISES

1. I (C) see hundreds (lit. "hairs of") of birds.
2. Your (C) tail is in the milk.
3. You (C) are taking a nap on your cushion.
4. My (C) eye is very sharp.
5. At night you (C) eat your dinner, and in the morning you have your tidbits.
6. Did you (C) eat the dog's food? (lit. You ate the not your food–dog. Remember not to use the 'arra form!)

8 FIELD TEST

Approach a strange Cat (one you have not tried to speak to before).[16] After an exchange of greetings, make a favorable comment about its appearance, intelligence, singing voice,

---

[16] It is only common sense, but some students do need to be told, not to approach a Cat who is engaged on business. A Cat studying birds, contemplating her name, or involved in purity ritual, for example, will have no time for a human communiCation, however flattering. If a Cat responds to your Flattery Voice communiCation with an Offended, or even Bored, Blink, *do not persist.* "Humans do not understand that a Cat who in human terms appears inactive may yet be too busy to speak to them." In this, Cats are not unlike writers.

or disposition, being sure to use the Flattery Voice. If the Cat responds, make another. Try to achieve a position where you retain the Cat's attention for five Flattery Voice observations. (Be imaginative! Nothing bores a Cat so fast as the same old "what fine whiskers you have!" and the like, day after day.)

Do not move on to Chapter Five until this has been achieved.

Chapter 5

IMPERATIVE

❖

THE FUTURE TENSE

❖

DIRECT AND INDIRECT OBJECTS

❖

EXPRESSIONS OF TIME

❖

NAMES

'Rowowmiuh   The Artist

mew(d4). mow 'aa a`bRah row.   Night. The Cat is in the bath-
mow ar(a1) truh a`bRah ruh(b2)   room. She is going to decorate the
mir(d1). mow me`a(a1) truh mir   bathroom with her claws. First,
'aa trrow(b1). mow meuh`a b'row   she sharpens her claws on the cur-
uh b'row maor(a5) mew(b4).   tains. Then she sculpts many yards
'Rowow 'Rowow row. ma`   of paper. It is very beautiful. The
maow(c4). ma`braa`(f7). mow   human comes in and sits down.
m`Row^(b1) ruh ma` prruh(b4).   The Cat reclines on its lap. "Stroke
mow miaow: *maaa`* *mow*   me," says the Cat. Meanwhile, the
Rup(c4). ma` meuh`a broh mow   human sees what the Cat has
pra mew(b4). ma`aaa`: *mow pra*   sculpted. "Cat," says the human,
truh a`bRah ruh maor(d1).   "you have decorated the bathroom
'Rowow row 'Rowow. wah uh wah   with artist's paper. How beautiful
a`bRah. RRow me`a maor nrow.   it is! What a pity there is not more
ma` aaa`(c4) brroh(d1) mew(d4)   of it." The human squeaks admir-
m`mew(a4).   ingly for a long time.

VOCABULARY

a`bRah(b1)	bathroom	mew(d4)	for a long time,
aaa`(c4)(nC)	to squeak, say	m`mew(a4)	"from night till
ar(a1)	intention		morning"
braa`(f 7)(nC)	to sit	mrrew(f 7)	name(nC)
brroh(a1)	admiringly, in	mrruh(d3)	name(C)
	admiration	pra^(b7)	sofa, firm claw
m`	to, for, at, from,		sharpener
	off, etc.	prruh(h4)(C)	to rest, recline; to
maor(d1)	paper, toilet/artist's		grace; to be at ease
	paper	Row^(b1)	lap, knee
maow(b4, c4)	to come, walk,	ruh(b2)	with, by means of
	move forward	Rup(c4)(nC)	to stroke, worship
me`a(a7)	first; now		through caress
meuh`a(a7)	second; then; after-	trrow(b1)	curtains, ladder,
	ward; meanwhile;		soft claw sharpener
	while	truh(b4, c4)	to stir, mix, pre-
mew(b4)(C)	decorate, rearrange,		pare; improve,
	sculpt; pull		adjust, knead, dec-
			orate; scratch;
			sharpen

1 THE IMPERATIVE

a. The imperative is formed by elongating the vowel of the pronoun **ma`** "you(nC)." The extended pronoun retains its BNTS (f 7).

maaa` pirp m`mow(a1) **maowr**(a4)   –   give me some
                                                       salmon

maaa` Rup**(c4) **mow ruh ma`row   –   stroke my fur

b. The extended pronoun also stands alone. It is a general instruction to cease some activity unpleasing to the Cat.

maaa`   –   cut it out!

c. There is no form of imperative for non-Cat use.[1] Humans may use their own language, such as English, to give an order to a Cat, but such commands are actually outside the comprehension area of most Cats.[2]

2 THE FUTURE TENSE

The future tense, called by Cats "the intention indiCator," is formed by inserting the future particle **ar** (a1, f 7) before the verb.

mow a`bRah ar(a1) **truh**   –   the Cat is going to decorate
                                                  the bathroom

ma` m`mow ar(f 7) **bra**   –   I (nC) will fetch you (some)
    birr birr   cream

---

[1] A form between Cats is in wide use, but there is no need for humans to know it. Any attempt on your part to use an imperative to a Cat would be a serious grammatical error. See Chapter Nine, Apology.

[2] And therefore, genuinely not heard. Antichat's views on this subject (expressed in a recent tabloid newspaper article) are both erroneous and invidious.

NOTE: Because it expresses intention, in certain situations it is inappropriate for humans to use the future tense. Do not use this construction to express such thoughts as, "I'm going to stroke you now," since this does not depend upon your intention but the Cat's.

mow ar prip m'ma' mow Rup — will you allow me to
stroke you?

3 DIRECT AND INDIRECT OBJECTS

A direct object is someone or something that directly receives the action of the verb. An indirect object receives the action only indirectly. In the sentence, "Rufus bit Fitz on the back leg," *Fitz* is the *direct object* of the verb *bit,* while *the back leg* is the *indirect object* governed by the preposition *on.*

a. There is no direct object marker. In ordinary statements direct objects follow the verb.

mow pra morh(b4) **mow Fitz** — I bit Fitz

Where the statement is emphatic, such as when an order is given or there is firm intent, the direct object may precede the action verb. It never precedes the imperative.

mupRup maor bra   – you must fetch more artist's paper
ma` birr ar bra *or*
   ma` ar bra birr(b5) – I will bring milk[3]

b. Indirect objects are signified by the preposition **m`** preceding the noun or pronoun.[4] It may mean "to, for, at" or any similar preposition in English. It always adopts the Begin Note of the word it precedes. Indirect objects generally precede the verb.

mow m`ma` ruh Row^   –   the Cat reclines on the
   prruh(b4)   human's lap
maaa` truh(c4)   –   stir (it) for me
   m`mow(a1)

c. It is not always easy to know whether an object is direct or indirect in Cat, and even fluent speakers often make mistakes. There is no rule, except to learn as you go. Generally speaking no apology is required for a mistake of this type.

mow pra morh mow   –   you bit Fitz on the paw *or* you
   Fitz ruh aw   bit Fitz's paw

---

[3] The former use is preferred because it puts the human in a laudable light. The Cat expression meaning "pie in the sky" is **birrmuhRRownpirpawama`**, lit. "an offer of milk that does not precede the verb."
[4] Do not confuse **m`** (indirect object marker) with **m'** the possessive particle.

4 EXPRESSIONS OF TIME

a. Expressions of time may stand alone.

mew(d4)   –   (it was) night(time)
mew(d4)   –   (it went on for) a long time (lit.
 m'mew(a4)   "from night till morning")

b. Where they form part of a longer sentence, they generally follow the subject.

mow me'a truh mir   – first, the Cat sharpens her claws

5 NAMES

Names are an extremely important area of Cat culture. There is, however, a high degree of secrecy surrounding the subject. That there is some actual function attached to names now seems clear, but what that function might be remains a mystery.

Some Cats may have more names than others, but if so, the reasons for this are unknown.[5] It seems possible that what humans call the Ordinary and Particular names[6] have both been invented solely for use by humans, although Cats do

---

[5] The ancient world, in particular the Egyptian priests, had a clearer understanding of these matters.
[6] See Eliot, *The Naming of Cats*, op. cit., p.1ff. Eliot listed three levels of name ("the name that the family use daily," the "name that's particular . . . that's more dignified," and "the name that no human research can discover"). Even if higher levels are proved to exist, his theory of the three tiers of name was groundbreaking, and must be considered correct in essentials. It is well worth study.

apparently sometimes use the Particular name among themselves. It is best not to engage in much discussion of names with any Cat you do not know extremely well. This text will restrict itself to a few forms for enquiring as to name.

a. Between Cats

Cats, much more than humans, require to know other Cats' names. It now seems certain that every Cat has at least some names beyond the Ordinary and Particular, and that these may be used only according to rigid rules regarding the relationship and level of intimacy subsisting between Cats. The methods of ascertaining the various names among Cats are apparently complex. Humans will rarely overhear these quasi-sacred formulas, and will never use them.

Cats never use, or enquire into, the Ordinary name among themselves. It is entirely for use with humans. However, some Cats nowadays do enquire as to another Cat's Particular name in the presence of humans, and for interest's sake, this form is given here.

mowuh ruh[7] **mrruh**   –   what is your Particular name?
mow(d4) **ruh rowb**(d1)   (lit. your name [is] God's
                                    tail tip)[8]

---

[7] Note that names are considered **attributes**.

[8] It has been suggested (Rechter, "Namen und 'Challenge'—neun frage," KS, Spring, 1991, pp. 112–38) that there is a long train of such questions, ending in the request to know the Cat's Most Secret Name. According to this theory, the final (ninth) question is "Your name is Divinity's Ninth Sensor." It is this phrase that is said to have given rise to the term "Cat's whiskers" in English, since the Ninth Sensor is also called The Whisker. This is very speculative.

b. Between Cat and Human

1. The formula for a human to ask a Cat's Ordinary name is new, and is a back formation from the above formula. Please remember the warning in Chapter One regarding the addressing of Cats. It would be an offense to ask a Cat who has not first addressed you what her name is.

mow(a1) **ruh mrruh**   – what is your Ordinary name?
   mow(d4) **ruh aw**(d1)   (lit. your name [is] God's paw)

Under no circumstances should you ever ask a Cat's Particular name. A Cat may volunteer this information, but any enquiry would be an offense. *It is for a Cat to initiate any change in the level of intimacy between Cat and human.*

2. Cats rarely ask humans their names. It is the highest form of compliment. The formula used is as follows.

ma` ruh mrrew(f 7) **'aa mow**   – your name (falls) within
   ruh brroh   God's shadow

The response to this is simply to state your name.[9]

---

[9] The old form of genuflection by stroking the tail tip as you speak your name is now considered very *passé*. Cats are extremely democratic and most prefer to let such old usages slide. However, if you should make the mistake of adopting the old form, and a Cat expresses disapproval, apology would be inappropriate.

NAMES AND INSULT

In a particularly bad mood, Cats sometimes use the form **'arra ma` ruh mrrew row?** (What the bleeping fleabag is your name?) This is meant as an insult. The best recourse is to pretend not to have heard. *Do not* respond to this question with your name. If you should happen to overhear one Cat put this question to another Cat, leave the vicinity if at all possible.

6   COMPREHENSION EXERCISE

mow m`ma` ruh(c7) Row^(b1) prruh(b4). mow a`bRah pra(c7) truh. mow me`a m`ma` ruh Row^ truh(b4). ma` meuh`a m`mow ruh ma`row Rup(c4). mow ar mRRow(b4).

7 PRACTICE EXERCISES

1. You (C) have decorated the bathroom. It is pretty.
2. You (C) were kneading the curtains.
3. Stroke me while I (C) take my ease on your lap.
4. The Cat is going to sculpt the toilet (artist's) paper.
5. The Cat is gracing the sofa with her presence.

8 REVIEW—PICK OUT THE ERRORS

Read the section below, picking out the grammatical errors and social solecisms. Then check your answers against the ones given below.

NOTE: **Do not read this section to your Cat.**

*Georgina, a Cat, and Marilyn, a human, have
never met before. Georgina is sitting on Marilyn's
garden fence, watching a butterfly. The butterfly
leaves, whereupon Georgina notices Marilyn, who
is standing quietly nearby.*

MOW:	**mow(a1).**
MA`:	**mow.***

Georgina presses her head against Marilyn's arm.

MOW:	**rrup.**
MA`:	**mow merowwap?****
MOW:	**moh.**
MA`:	**'arra m'mow mrrew row?*****

*Georgina involuntarily claws Marilyn, taking care
to spoil her new cashmere sweater.*

ANSWERS

* Although grammatically **mow** is an acceptable response to
the greeting **mow**, in practice, where a human meets a Cat
for the first time, **ma`** is more precise. It indiCates a general
character of willingness to be of service to the Cat, and thus
promotes good interspecies relations.

**Although no offer of food is taken amiss, Marilyn should
not have ignored Georgina's Invitation to Intimacy. The correct response is a communiCation in the Flattery Voice.

When two or three such comments have been accepted, time enough to go on to the offer of food.

***This is an extreme grammatical, syntactical, and social solecism. Did you recognize the triple error? Marilyn's first error is social—she has instigated a discussion of names before Georgina has indiCated any interest in the subject. Her second error is syntactical—she has used **mrrew,** which is restricted to non-Cat names. Her third error is by far the most serious: she uses the question form **'arra.** This error is rendered even more egregious because it pertains to a Cat's name. Of course it is unlikely that any Cat, however provoked, would react in the manner stated. It is put here to make you aware of the enormity of the insult in human terms. Marilyn will probably be under an embargo[11] by Cats for some time.

[11] An embargo of this type is not now and never has been called a "Catwa." This is a joke that has gone far enough.

Chapter 6

COLOR NAMES

◆

HERE AND THERE

◆

HERE IS, THERE IS

◆

THIS AND THAT

◆

COMPARISON

◆

ATTENTION

mowmew	The Kittens

mow Minou 'aa 'aiou(a4) prruh(b4). mow m`mowmew(d2) m'ow(b2) miaow.

Minou is lying in her basket. She speaks softly to her kittens.

ma` broh brroh m`mowmew. mia'. bRuh(c4) Rup mowmew.[1] mow mowruh mbruuh.

The human is admiring the kittens. Its attention is pleasant. It wants to stroke the kittens. Minou graciously grants permission.

ma` mowmew brrow(d1) morih(c4). mowmew brrow miaow: *mew*(d4).

The human picks up the kitten of white coat with six black hairs on his occiput. "Mew," says the kitten.[2]

aaa`: *mowmew brrow mowruh*(d4) *row!* mowmew brrow Rup(c4). mowmew brrow moreh(c4). mowmew friuh(d2) morih.

"He is adorable," says the human. It strokes the white kitten[3] and puts it down. It picks up the black kitten with white nose, breast, and three paws, excluding the right forepaw.

aaa`: *nr'mow mowmew mboh mboh mowmew brroh row.*

"This kitten is bigger than the white one," it remarks.

mow maow miaow: *ow ow nmbruh.*

Minou gently warns,[4] "Comparisons are invidious."

aaa` preh'(c1): *mowmew 'Rowow row 'Rowow 'Rowow. mowmew 'Rowow ruh mow*(d4).

"They are all most beautiful," says the human hastily. "Each is as beautiful as Mow."[5]

---

[1] Alert students will wonder why the direct object here does not precede the verb, since the intention must of course be very high. This is because it is inappropriate for the human to have a firm intention to stroke the kittens before the Cat has given permission.

[2] Lit. "The kitten speaks the Sacred Word." By tradition, all kittens speak a mysterious sacred word that adult Cats can neither speak nor understand. It is assumed that this sound is the Central Note of the Universe.

[3] Through considerations of space, the full descriptions of Cat coat colors are not repeated.

[4] Lit. "speaks in Second Maow." See Chapter Eight.

[5] A common expression used of kittens when speaking to the Mother Cat.

VOCABULARY

'aiou(a4)	bed; basket; wash-tub; drawer	merah(b4)	house
^ra`(b1)	toy	moreh(c4)(nC)	to put down
breh(b2)	tree	morih(c4)(nC)	to pick up
breh(c2)	wall	m'ow(b2)	softly, gently
brrow(d1)	white with blue eyes, six black hairs on the occiput	mow(b3)	good
		mowmew(d2)	kitten, kittens
bru(d2)	white, no markings	mowruh(d3)	adorable, worthy of adoration/ worship
frah(d4)	black, no markings		
friuh(d2)	black with white nose, breast and three paws, the right fore black	mrah(d1)	cream with dark nose, paws, and tail tip
		mrah(d2)	gray, no markings
irr(a5)	delicious	mrah(d4)	tabby, no white
maaa(a4)	floor	mruh(d4)	ginger, no white
maow(a7) miaow(b4)	to warn gently	nr'mow(a1)	there
		preh(c1)	quickly
mboh(c5)	big	pwah(a1) (C)	to dislike, disdain
		r'mow(a1)	here

1 COLOR NAMES

Cat is very rich in color descriptive words. Cats do not recognize anything resembling what humans call "breed" among Cats. No generic term for "Siamese," "Tabby," "Burmese," etc., exists in the language. Instead, there are almost as many words to describe types of fur coloring as there are Cats.

For example, there are at least four words to describe identically striped tabbies according to how wide the central stripe running along the spine is, and many different terms for white Cats with various single and multiple markings.

It is virtually impossible for a human being to learn all these various descriptive words, particularly as some of the distinguishing characteristics are not visible to the human apparatus.[6] This chapter gives you several basic color terms, and you may wish, by a challenge question, to use the term closest to your own Cat to determine the correct word.

If your Cat is ginger, for example, the question,

mow mruh(d4) **row** – are you a ginger Cat (without
white markings)?

may elicit some such response as

mow ufrah(d1) **row** – I have orange and ochre inter-
mingled stripes, white
forepaws, variegated hindpaws,
a broad white breast patch
running to a point between
the forelegs; the tip of the tail
deep ochre.

---

[6] It is complete nonsense to imagine, as some scientists do, that Cats do not perceive color. In fact, Cats have a more sensitive eye than humans. In addition to the "human" spectrum, Cats perceive colors in a spectrum that (in allegorical terms) runs at 90 degrees to it.

Once a Cat has imparted its Color Name to you, be sure to learn it. It is an offense to use a wrong Color Name twice (see Chapter Nine).[7]

2 HERE AND THERE

By now you should have begun to appreciate that the world-view of Cats is fundamentally different from our own. This difference appears again when we search for a way of expressing the English concepts "here" and "there." In English, generally, when we say "here," we mean "close to me (the speaker) or to the position in space that I am inhabiting." "There" usually means "far from me (the speaker) or the space I am inhabiting, in a particular direction."

In Cat, **r'mow** (a1) and **nr'mow** (a1)—"here" and "there"—are always *relative to the position of the Cat*, regardless of who is speaking. If you remember that the literal translation of these terms is "in Cat's presence" and "not in Cat's presence," you will find it easier to keep the distinctions in mind.

a. When a Cat is speaking, the terms are straightforward.

mRaow r'mow nrow(a1)   –   (my) food is not here (i.e., not near me[C])

maaa` nr'mow moreh(c4)   –   put it there

---

[7] Much as with humans, Color Names may be used between Cats as terms of abuse. This involves altering the BNTS of the Color Name. Therefore be very careful about accepting from one Cat a Color Name for another Cat. Get your information straight from the Cat's tongue.

b. When a human is speaking

1. **When Cat and human are in close proximity,** as for example, when your knee is occupied by a Cat, "here" for you will naturally be **r'mow,** since you yourself are in the Cat's presence. It follows that anything not close to you, "there," is also "not in the Cat's presence," **nr'mow.**

ma` r'mow row   –   I (nC) am here (with you)[8]

2. **When the human and Cat are not in close proximity,** often a human speaker of Cat may simply *reverse* these words. Thus, "here" will generally mean "not in Cat presence," **nr'mow,** since what is close to you will not be close to the Cat, and "there" will be "in Cat presence," **r'mow,** if it is close to the Cat. If you are speaking of an object or place not close to you *and* not close to the Cat you are addressing, you would naturally use the form **nr'mow,** "not in Cat's presence."

c. "There" has greater force in English than **nr'mow.** Most things that are **nr'mow** are of no interest to a Cat, and indeed the word is often used to express a Cat's lack of interest in something.[9] If you were to say to a Cat **mRaow(b3) row**(a1) **nr'mow**(a1), "(Your) food is there," the word **nr'mow** will have much the same force and meaning as does

---

[8] There are strong overtones to this apparently simple statement that tend to make it pleasing to Cats. Literally, "the non-Cat is in the presence of Cat," it communiCates a sense of being honored and a gratitude almost epiphany that are not obvious in the English.
[9] Cf. the English "neither here nor there."

"there" in the English sentence. However, the sentence, "The dog is there," **awa row nr'mow,** does not carry the meaning, as it does in English, "The dog is in a specific, indiCated place." It would mean simply, "The dog is of no interest."

3 HERE IS, HERE ARE

"Here is" in English is relatively closely translated by the Cat **ma` pirp r'mow,** "I offer into Cat's presence."

birr pirp r'mow   –   here is your milk

This also serves for plural constructions.

mRRah mRRah pirp r'mow   –   here are a few tidbits

Where the meaning is not emphatic, the verb **row** is used.

Johnny row(a1)   –   here's Johnny (lit. "it's Johnny")

4 THERE IS, THERE ARE

Where the meaning is not emphatic, the verb **row** is used.

mowmew 'aa 'aiou(a4) **row**   –   there are kittens in the
                                        basket

Where the meaning is emphatic, the construction is more difficult. For ordinary conversational purposes it is best to avoid this construction. Remember that anything not close to a Cat is rarely of interest unless it is making sounds or movement that will announce its own presence.

For example, **marr**(a5) **nr'mow**(a1) **row**, ostensibly "There's a bird," may be spoken by a Cat in certain situations, but the expression will then carry overtones of intent as well as interest. It would be inappropriate for you ever to announce the presence of a bird at a distance, since any Cat's powers of perception in such matters far surpass your own, and you would be guilty of the peculiarly human sin, roundly disliked by Cats, called ^^^**ow**(f 7) "redundancy" or "unnecessariness."[10] See Chapter Nine, Apology.

5 THIS AND THAT

The English "this" and "that" are expressed by **r'mow** and **nr'mow**, "here" and "there."

mowmew nr'mow	– this kitten (i.e., the one not near
'Rowow row	you the Cat) is beautiful

6 COMPARISON

Cats consider comparison invidious. Avoid comparing one Cat with another. A simple statement such as **mow 'Rowow row**—"You are pretty"—will always be sufficient; there is no

---

[10] In the case of an old or infirm Cat, the insult of pointing out, for example, a bird whose presence the Cat has not detected should be avoided at all costs.

need whatsoever to attempt any such construction as, for example, "You are the most beautiful Cat in the world." Any mention of a Cat not present to one who is is somewhat insulting (see Chapter Four). To mention *all the other Cats in the world* would deeply offend any normally sensitive Cat. (See Chapter Nine, Apology.)

a. The Repetitious or Self-Defined Comparative
Of course, you will frequently want to express the thought that a particular Cat is, as it were, "more than pretty." This is achieved by intensifying, that is, through the means of doubling or bracketing of adjectives described in Chapter Two.

'Rowow mow 'Rowow	– more than pretty Cat
mow(b3) maow(d4) mow(b3)	– a better song

b. The Self-Defined Superlative
A triple repetition of the adjective is the equivalent of the English superlative[11] and as a construction is generally very welcome to most Cats.

'Rowow mow 'Rowow	– you are the prettiest Cat!
'Rowow row	*or* you are as pretty as
	pretty can be[12]

---

[11] Cf. the archaic English "thrice-pretty Cat."
[12] Not "as pretty as a Cat can be," since by definition there is no limit to how pretty— or anything else—a Cat can be.

NOTE: It is quite permissible to combine the repetitious comparative or superlative with the Flattery Voice.

mow 'R<u>owow</u> row 'R<u>owow</u> – you certainly are one
 'R<u>owow</u>   supremely beautiful Cat

c. "True" Comparative and Superlative

These forms are used rarely, and only in a purely descriptive and above all nonjudgmental way, with reference to inanimate objects. *All judgmental comparisons should be left to Cats.*

POSITIVE	COMPARATIVE	SUPERLATIVE
adjective	ow(a7) + adjective	ow(a7) ow(a7) + adjective
big	bigger	biggest
mboh (c5)	**ow mboh**	**ow ow mboh**

NOTE: The most common use of the true comparative and superlative among Cats is for insult. As the author can attest from personal experience, even a simple statement such as

mow ruh ma`row ow frah(d4)   –   your coat is darker
 row Blacky   than Blacky's

may be taken as a grave insult. Although the point is not yet quite clear, it seems that, when directed at sentient individuals, **ow** may have a pejorative connotation. It is safer to use the repetitious comparative.

breh(b2) **mboh mboh row** – the tree is bigger than the
  merah(b4)   house

7 A NOTE ON ATTENTION

Cats divide attention into Positive or Pleasant Attention,
mia'(d4), and Negative or Uncomfortable Attention, **pra'**
(f 7). Both types of attention are within the Cat visibility
range, occurring along the sensation/color spectrum—
mrrowa(d1)—which runs perpendicularly to our spectrum. This spectrum extends beyond the visual into other
senses. (As indeed do the extremes of our spectrum, the fla-
vor/color/sensation spectrum—**mrroh**(d1): beyond ultravi-
olet is a sweetish bone flavor, for example; beyond infrared
there is a light stroking sensation.) In the **mrrowa** spectrum, Positive Attention has what has variously been
described as a "warm" or "musical" color/tone. Negative
Attention has an unpleasantly scratchy or buzzing color.

It is not at all easy for humans to control the nature of
their attention. A too-eager human who feels entirely positive feelings toward a Cat is nevertheless capable of extending highly uncomfortable Negative Attention. This is particularly true of children.

The easiest way of getting the feel of Positive Attention is
to monitor yourself when reading a *reasonably interesting*
newspaper article. Cats trying to train humans will often
come and sit in this attention, which is extremely pleasant.

This is the color of attention Cats like best. The crinkle of newsprint as the Cat reclines on it adds an attractive note to the color melody.

8 COMPREHENSION EXERCISE

mow bru(d2) **row**(a1)? **mupRup broh**(c4) **mow**(b3) **mow**(b3). **mow brrow**(d1) **row. mowmew**(d2) **mowmew**(d2) **mowruh**(d3) **'aa 'aiou**(a4) **mRRow**(b4). **ma` pirp r'mow ^ra`**(1).

9 PRACTICE EXERCISE

1. Here is a big mouse.
2. A mouse is nicer than a toy.
3. Is cream whiter than milk?
4. Dogs are boring (lit. "Dogs are there").
5. You are the prettiest Cat in Christendom. (Careful!)
6. Don't you (C) like your food?

10 PRACTICAL EXERCISES WITH A NATIVE
SPEAKER

On Sunday morning, when the Cat is in the room or on the bed with you, spread open whatever section of the Sunday paper interests you. Choose an item of reasonable but not extreme interest and read it. Read for five minutes. Has the Cat come to sit in your attention? If not, perhaps the item you are reading has excited you too much or not enough. Choose another.

When the Cat comes and sits on the paper between your eyes and the words you were reading, pause to note exactly how much and what kind of attention you were extending as you read. Trying to keep up this exact degree of attention, switch the *object* of your attention to the Cat.

If the Cat begins to purr, you have achieved a state of Positive Attention. Practice giving this kind of attention to your Cat.

At times when you want the Cat's company but the Cat is otherwise engaged, rather than subject the Cat to demanding and possibly Negative Attention, it is useful to turn the attention you have practiced onto something else, such as a book or paper. You may find the Cat is not so busy after all!

Chapter 7

THE FANTASY VOICE

◆

NUMBERS

◆

THE SUBORDINATE CONNECTOR

◆

THE UNIVERSAL IT

◆

IMPERSONAL CLASS THREE VERBS

MIAOWMEUH(a4)	DIALOGUE
MOW: **mow**(a1) **ma`ar miaow. mut.**	I am going to tell you (something). Listen carefully.
MA`: **ma`**(f 7).	I'm all ears.
MOW: **mboh mowruh**(E5) **mboh.**	A very big secret.
MA`: **ma`**(f 7)!	Yes, yes!
MOW: **mow**(a1) **ma` pra nmiaow muh**(a7) **mow broh**(a1) **arruh**(E5).	I haven't told you before that Cats see the future.
MA`: **ma` nrow**(c4) **rrow**(a3).	I beg your pardon?
MOW: (speaks slowly) **mow broh arruh**(E5).	Cats see the future.
MA`: (excitedly) **moh**(a5).	Do they really?
MOW: **moh**(E5). **mew mow ma` miaow meuh**(E4) **ruh mowrow**(c4).	Yes. I can tell you the winning lottery numbers tonight.
MA`: **mbruh mboh!**	Fantastic!
MOW: **mupRup moreh**(c4) **b'row uh b'row mRRah**(E3).	You must put a lot of money into it . . .

VOCABULARY

arruh(a5)	future, the future	**muah**(c3)	ticket
b'row uh b'row	"hairs of," i.e., lots of, many	**muh**(a7)	when, nevertheless, and, but, however, who, which, etc.; the subordinate connector
meuh(d4)	numbers		
mirr(C4)(nC)	to purchase, bring for approval, buy	**mut**(a7)	listen! pay attention!
moh(a5)	yes; indeed?	**nrow**(c4)	"to have no whiskers," to be stu-
moh(a5) **row**(a1, f7)	to believe (be in a state of belief)	**rrow**(b3)(nC)	pid, to beg pardon for not hearing
mowrow(c4)	winning, lucky (lit. "Cat-having")	**rowb maar** (b4, d1)	to be angry, to storm, to lash one's tail
mowruh(a5)	secret; Catlike	**urr**(b4,c4)	to choose
mrow(d1, b4)	to do, take, make		
mRRah(a3)	money		

1 THE FANTASY VOICE

Cats have a lively sense of humor. This may cause difficul-
ties for more stolid species, such as humans, who should
always be wary whenever a Cat divulges strange or unusual
information to them (see Introduction).

Fortunately, their spirit of fair play means that Cats do
not keep and entirely straight face when joking: they use
the Fantasy Voice. The careful listener need not fear being
made what Cats call "one of BRRow's minions."

Study this section closely.[1]

---

[1] The author shall not be held responisble for any act of wit or humor, or any joke,
practical or otherwise, perpetrated by any Cat on any human or member of any other
species whatsoever as a result of their study of this book.

HOW IT WORKS

The Fantasy Voice is extremely simple to detect once you know what to look for. It is indiCated by a change in the Begin Note of some or all of the nouns in an exchange. Whatever the natural Begin Note of the word, it shifts to E. The Tonal Shape remains unchanged.

mow broh arruh(a5)   –   Cats can see the future

mow broh arruh(E5)   –   Cats can see the future (*nudge, nudge, wink, wink!*)

FANTASY AND HUMAN ETIQUETTE

There are two ways of responding when you are in doubt as to the factual basis of what you have been told.

a. ask to have the information repeated (so that you can listen more closely)

ma` nrow rrow   –   I beg your pardon? (lit. I have no whiskers)[2]

---

[2] This is a simple recognition of the fact that whiskers are a "sense" that humans do not have, and not, as Dogfodder suggests, an impliCation that anyone without whiskers is intellectually below par. Cats often say that they are able to detect the Fantasy Voice with their whiskers.

b. use the "moh" challenge

moh (a5) – really? [3]

Again, you must listen closely to the response. If the reply is **moh**[4] using the BNTS E5, you are meant to appreciate the Cat's imaginative storytelling, but not to take all that she says literally.

NOTE: *High levels of excitement tend to render humans deaf to the subtle shift to Fantasy Voice. Be very very careful whenever a Cat tells you something that engages your extreme interest.*[5]

HUMAN USE OF THE FANTASY VOICE

Naturally you will be eager to use the Fantasy Voice yourself. Although grammatically it is acceptable, humans should attempt the Fantasy Voice only when they are sure a Cat is in the mood for a joke.

Do not use the Fantasy Voice to discuss a food offering that you do not actually mean to give to the Cat. This is a grammatical offense of an extremely high order (see Chapter Nine, Apology). Never, for example, say

---

[3] This means literally "belief" and is short for ma` **moh row**(f 7), "I believe it."

[4] Short for **maaa` moh row**(f 7)—(believe it!)

[5] Hundfress's contention that, *'wenn Sie Sich an etwas sehr interessieren, kommt die Fantasiestimme nicht'* (*KS*, Summer 1993, pp. 34–44) is utterly groundless. There is no example of an attested deliberate omission of the Fantasy Voice on record, in spite of numerous attempts to catch Cats out.

ma` m`mow mew pirp – tonight I am going to let
marr(E5)   you eat the canary for din-
                                 ner (ho ho!)

2 MEUH (NUMBERS)

Counting is based on three and nine. The numbers one to
nine are given here. For the higher numbers, the student is
referred to *Cat Grammar*.

one   **me** (a2)
two   **meuh** (a2)
three **uhmeuh** (a3)
four   **uhmeuh**(a3) **me**(a2)
five   **uhmeuh**(a3) **meuh**(a2)
six   **uhmeuh**(a3) **uhmeuh**(a3)
seven **uhmeuh**(a2)
eight **uhmeuh**(a2) **me**(a2)
nine   **uhmeuh** (d4)

1. The numbers three and nine are considered sacred.

2. Numbers, like adjectives, may precede, follow, or
bracket the noun to which they refer. Nouns defined by
numbers are singular.

six tidbits   –   **uhmeuh**(a3) **mRRah**(a4) **uhmeuh**(a3)

or

uhmeuh(a3) **uhmeuh**(a3) **mRRah**

3. You may be surprised to hear a Cat singing numbers. This is connected with the sacred mystery of numbers, and cannot be further explained to humans at this time.[6] It is an offense for a non-Cat to sing numbers.

NOTE: Because the Cat sense of humor is particularly activated around numbers, it is usually best not to ask a Cat for important phone numbers, for example.

3 THE SUBORDINATE CONNECTOR

When two or more ideas are in a dependent relationship, they are joined by **muh**(f 7).

mow muh merowwap   –   when a Cat is hungry, she
 mRaow bRuh   wants food

mow ruh rowb pwah   –   the Cat with the wet tail,
 muh ma` pra bRRow(c4)   whom you tricked, is not
 nbRRow(a1)   laughing

---

[6] Humans have already done more than enough damage with numbers.

mow miaow muh marr –   I (C) said that the canary
   irr row(a1)[7]   was delicious

4 THE UNIVERSAL IT

a. Passive Voice

1. The English passive voice is rendered by the use of the non-Cat form of the verb without any subject.

meuh pra urr(c4) – the numbers were chosen

2. Cat action is not normally rendered in the passive.

mow pra brap marr(a5)   –   the bird was eaten by the
                                   Cat (the Cat ate the bird)

3. There is one example of the Cat passive used by humans:

ma` RRow (a1)   –   I am blessed

It serves as an expression of extreme gratitude, generally after an apology has been accepted. See Chapter Nine, Apology.

[7.] Note that the canary, being considered food by the time of being eaten, takes the Cat form of the verb. In a sentence such as **mow miaow muh marr 'Rowow row**(f 7), "I said that the canary was attractive," the (nC) verb is of course used.

b. Active Voice

The universal it may be used by humans as an alternate to the first person, by dropping the subject **ma`**.

m'mow mRRah pra	– I bought your tidbits (your tid-
mirr (c4)	bits have been bought)

This form of all non-Cat verbs is syntactically preferable, since Cats do not distinguish human personality in quite the way we do.[8] Cats will often leave out the pronoun when speaking to you.

pra mirr b'row uh b'row	– did you buy lots of (lottery)
muah(c3)	tickets?

It is an offense, however, to leave out the pronoun "you" when you are addressing a Cat. See Chapter Nine, Apology.

mow pra maaow m' mow	– your milk was spilled on the
birr 'aa maaa	floor (by you)

5 IMPERSONAL CLASS THREE VERBS

As in English and many other languages, there are certain impersonal verbs used to describe action not performed by anyone, e.g., "it is raining."

---

[8] It is also admired for being self-effacing, something Cats approve of in humans.

These are rendered as if they were "Acts of Mow." These verbs carry the BNTS D1, which indiCates neither action nor state of being, but something between the two. They are always preceded by **mow**(d4), "the Goddess."

mow(d4) **rro**(d1)   – it is raining (lit. Mow washes)
mow RRooww(d1)   – it is pleasant (lit. Mow purrs)
mow rowb maar(d1) – it is stormy (lit. Mow lashes her tail)

SOME UNEXPECTED CLASS THREE VERBS

Certain other verbs also take the Mow form.

mow(d4) **mrow**(d1) –   it has disappeared (lit. Mow has taken it)
mow bRRow(d1)   –   it is ridiculous (lit. Mow is laughing)
mow RRah(d1)   –   it is offensive, *or* it is dangerous (lit. Mow blinks slowly)
mow frah(d1)   –   it is dark

Many Class Three impersonal verbs also exist as Class One and Two perfect verbs; that is, there is no non-Cat form of the verb. In this book these verbs are notated (d1, a1) and (d1, b4).

6 COMPREHENSION EXERCISE

ma` moh row muh mow ruh rrow(b3) mowrow row? nrow rrow. marr(E5) brap 'aa m'mow Row(E4). mow(d4) rro muh mow 'aa mi'ao(a4) miaow(b4). mew(d4) pra mow frah uh rowb maar(d1).

7 TRANSLATE

1. Is that so?
2. That's unbelievable!
3. Do Cats see in the dark?
4. How ridiculous that the human believed what the Cat said about the future. The Cat was joking, but humans are stupid.
5. It is dangerous to play tricks when a Cat is engaged in the purity ritual.

8 PRACTICAL EXERCISES WITH A NATIVE SPEAKER

Playing BRRow

Hide your Cat's dinner, and tell her that she has eaten it already, plate and all. Has she recognized your use of the Fantasy Voice? If so, she will say, **bRRow**. If not, continue to play the joke. After she has protested several times, if she still does not Catch on, reveal your joke and say **bRRow(d1)**. (Do not prolong the joke beyond two or three exchanges.)

NOTE: If your Cat responds to this attempt to play BRRow with the Offended Blink, give a hasty start as if remembering that you have put it somewhere, and produce her food with no more ado. *Do not admit to having used the Fantasy Voice or apologize for playing BRRow.* Pretend that the whole thing has been a simple mistake.

Chapter 8

THE OFFENDED VOICE

◆

THE GENTLE REPROACH

◆

EARLY WARNING

◆

EFFECTIVE RESPONSES TO EARLY WARNING

mow
uh urrt pirp maow

The Cat and the Child
Who Gave Offense

mow 'aa pra^ row uh urrt. mow rro rowb. mow maowrow(b4). urrt aaa`: *mow.*

A Cat and a child are on the sofa. The Cat is cleaning her tail. She is singing. The child says, "Cat."

mow mowruh nprih(b4). mow mra'.

The Cat tolerantly does not hear. She carries on with her work.

urrt mow Rup(c4). urrt mow ruh ma`row truh(c4). mow broh(b4) urrt uh nbroh(b4).

The child touches the Cat. It ruffles the Cat's coat. The Cat blinks the Offended Blink at the child.

urrt mow ruh prih(d2) owuh(c4). mow miaow: *maaa`.* uh(f 7) urrt 'aw. urrt ma` row. rrow nrow.

The child pulls the Cat's ear. The Cat says, "Stop that." But the child continues. It is non-Cat. It is stupid.

mow maow(a7) miaow: (-2) *maaaaa`.* urrt mow ruh rowb owuh.

The Cat says irritably, "Cut that out!" The child pulls the Cat's tail.

mow m`ma` mboh maow(c7) miaow: (-4) $\overline{mow}$ rruh rro̅wb urrrrt (f3) $\overline{owuh}$(c4)!

The Cat complains to the adult human, "The child is pulling my tail!"

ma` mboh rrow nrow nprih(c4).

The whiskerless adult non-Cat does not hear.

mow truh(b4) urrt. urrt maa`row. me'a ma` mboh maow(c4). ma` aaa`: *RRow!*(c6)

The Cat scratches the child. The child sings. Now the adult human comes. "What a pity!" it squeaks.

mow mah(b4) m`pra^. mow mowruh mah(b4).

The Cat gets down from the sofa and majestically departs.

VOCABULARY

'aw(c4)(nC)	to continue a displeasing act
broh(b4) uh nbroh(b4)	to "look and not look"; i.e., to blink at; give the Offended Blink
maa`row(c4)(nC)	to sing[1]
mah(b4, c4)	to leave, depart; vaCate
maow(a7) miaow(b4)(C)	to speak in Second Maow
maow(c7) miaow(b4)(C)	to speak in Fifth Maow
maow pirp(c4)(nC)	to give offense to, insult
marr(a5)	canary; bird with strong, interesting odor
mra'(b4)(C)	to continue, carry on, carry out (usu. ritual)
owuh(c4)(nC)	to pull, squeeze, cause irritation to
praowme`a(f3)	Early Warning
prih(b4, c4)	to hear, listen
prih(d2)	ear
RRow(c6)	oversight, error; My Goodness! or What a pity!
uh(f 7)	but, although
urrt(f3)	child, offspring, cub (nC)

1 THE OFFENDED VOICE

Everything that you have been taught so far in this book is in NMaow, the Benign or Unoffended Voice, sometimes

---

[1] This is the closest Cat can come to the English "whine" or "complain." It is inappropriate for humans to feel or express disapproval of Cats, and Cats actually do not hear human plaint.

called First Maow. You yourself will confine all communi-
Cation to this voice. Cats, however, have access also to
Maow, the Offended Voice, and it is essential that you learn
to understand it.

Although grammatically there are said to be seven
degrees of Maow, *practically* there are six. No one can say
exactly why NMaow, the Unoffended Voice, occupies the
position of first degree of offense, as Cats have so far not
explained the matter.

The six levels of Maow—called by Cats **trrow(b1)
maow(f1)**—the Ladder of Offense—all imply that something has occurred to offend the Cat. In the lower degrees,
this may very often be a grammatical solecism on the part
of a nonnative speaker.[2] Except at the extreme end—Sixth
and Seventh Maow—the degrees are hard for the beginner
to distinguish.[3] Learn to listen carefully.

Grammatically, each degree of Maow requires its corre-
sponding level of apology, and to offer a lower level of apology than the Maow used is an insult (see Chapter Nine). It
is best to forestall the rapid shift up the Ladder of Maow—
which generally occurs when there is an inadequate
response—by responding quickly with the correct level of
apology.

---

[2] Cats are, however, extremely understanding and tolerant, and will often overlook lesser
grammatical solecisms on the part of a beginner because they understand how difficult
the language is for the limited human apparatus.
[3] The levels have specific names in Cat, but they are difficult and not really necessary to
the beginner. Those interested may consult *Cat Grammar.*

STRUCTURE

The Offended Voice involves changes in four areas: nasality, vowel length, the r and R consonants, and Begin Note; in Sixth and Seventh Maow there are also changes in vocabulary and syntax.

a. **Second Maow**—The vowels are elongated and somewhat nasalised. Only practice will acclimatize your ear to these subtle variations in sound.

mow (a1) merowwap (a1) — I am (still) waiting for my
food

b. **Third Maow**—Vowels elongated and nasalized, as above. Begin Notes of entire communiCation drop one point. At this level a Cat will usually name the offense.

(-1) nmupRup m'mā' — you (nC) must not call yourself
pirp mrrew mow   Mow

c. **Fourth Maow**—Glottal R and RR become palatal r and rr respectively. Increased nasalization. Increased vowel length. Begin Note one to three points lower than Third Maow. Used in situations of physical discomfort, or where too much or not enough attention is being repeatedly offered.

(-2) m$\overline{\text{aaa}}$` m$\overline{\text{awrow}}$(b6) **bra**(c4)!　–　open this door!

d. Fifth Maow—Palatal **rr** becomes vowelized **r**,[4] loses the friCative and is elongated. Begin Note one to three points lower than Fourth Maow. Vowelization and nasalization as for Fourth Maow. Used in situations of grammatical, social, physical, and mental irritation.

(-4) **m$\overline{\text{ow}}$ ruh rr$\overline{\text{ow}}$b urrrrt**(f3)　–　the child is pulling
　　$\overline{\text{ow}}$uh(c4)　　　　　　　　　　　　my tail

e. Sixth Maow—**R** and **RR** become heavily elongated vowelized **r**. Heavy nasalization and vowel elongation. Begin Note plummets. At this level syntax becomes distorted, and word meaning alters (often becoming intensified). Much doubling and bracketing of adjectives. Used in situations of extreme annoyance.

(-8) **'arrrra nmbrrrruh $\overline{\text{aw}}$**　–　you are standing on my
　　m$\overline{\text{a}}$`[5] **nmbrrrruh $\overline{\text{awa}}$ $\overline{\text{awa}}$**　　　tail (lit. what the bleep
　　m`mow rrrr$\overline{\text{ow}}$b　　　　　　very nasty paw non-Cat
　　　　　　　　　　　　　　　　　dog dog my tail?)

---

[4] Notated by **rrr+**.
[5] Note the absence of attribute marker **ruh**.

f. Seventh Maow—Almost incomprehensible to humans, except in intent. Begin Note, Tonal Shape, syntax, and vocabulary completely at variance with ordinary speech. Nasalization extreme. Use of the glottal hiss. Used to express fury and threats.[6]

USE

The Offended Voice may be used only by a Cat.
As mentioned above, humans and other non-Cats are grammatically confined to the use of NMaow. You must not try to use Maow to indiCate that you are annoyed by something a Cat may or may not have done. This is a gross grammatical solecism. (See Chapter Nine, Apology.) Remember that grammar is not separable from social situations in Cat. If something is troubling you, express yourself in NMaow.

mow maor(a5) mew(b4) – Cats enjoy pulling toilet
   mbruh row uh   paper down but sadly it
   nmbruh row   makes an awful mess

mow pra brap marr(a5) – what a pity you mistook the
   RRow   canary for your dinner

---

[6] It is impossible to represent Seventh Maow in the Roman alphabet. Those who are interested may see *Cat Grammar*.

THE DIRECT RESPONSE

At any level of Maow a Cat who has reason to believe that remonstrance is useless may abandon the Ladder of Offense and have recourse to the Direct Response, that is, biting or scratching or both.

2 THE GENTLE REPROACH

Sadly, the judging of the particular level of Maow in any instance is not quite so simple a matter as the above seems to indiCate. In Chapter One you have already been introduced to what Cats call the Gentle Reproach, but which humans tend to term the Offended Blink.[7] At the lower levels of Maow, this blink, roughly speaking, may be considered the equivalent of one degree of Maow. An Offended Blink on its own is usually taken to be Second Maow; an Offended Blink accompanied by a communiCation in Second Maow is obviously, therefore, not Second Maow but Third Maow; similarly a communiCation in Third Maow accompanying the Offended Blink is in effect a Fourth Maow communiCation.[8]

3 EARLY WARNING

Most Cats, of course, prefer not to put a human into a situ-

---

[7] A slow blink followed by turning the head away.

[8] Here the effect ceases, however. The Gentle Reproach never accompanies the higher degrees of offense. As Cats explain, it would be no favor to humans to reprimand with a milder form of reproach than the grammatical or other error deserves, for then how would we learn the right way?

ation where apology and groveling become necessary. They give what are called Early Warnings, **praowme`a(f3)**, where they perceive a human about to fall into error. A careful human will not concentrate on the linguistic formulas to the exclusion of ordinary observance of Cat signals.

a. The Tail Tip Twitch—a Cat, sitting upright, her tail extended behind or wrapped around her lower limbs, twitches the tail tip slightly when she perceives a human about to commit a Maow-level offense.

b. The Irritated Purr—A short burst of rough purring, possibly accompanied by pressure of the Cat's head against some part of a human's body, is a warning that the Fourth Maow offense of Too Little Attention is being offered the Cat.

c. The Extended Paw—The Cat extends the Paw of Intimacy to indiCate to the human that the offense of Failure to Make a Food Offering When Appropriate may be occurring.

4 EFFECTIVE RESPONSES TO EARLY WARNINGS

In most cases where a Cat gives Early Warning, an immediate, heartfelt communiCation in the Flattery Voice, accompanied by any small offering of food,[9] will usually put the situation to rights.

---

[9] In most instances whatever the human itself happens to be eating will be adequate.

mow 'R<u>owow</u> <u>row</u>   –   how handsome you are!

mRaow   –   would you like a taste?

5 COMPREHENSION EXERCISES

urrt r'mow rrow nrow. mow uhmeuh(a3) praowme'a pra prip.
mow me`a maow(a7)   miaow. ma` nprih(c4). ma` prih(d2)
row? moh, prih row. RRow nprih.

6 PRACTICE

1. Has the human insulted you?
2. The child has pulled her ear, her tail, and her
   whiskers. She is extremely patient.
3. The Cat wisely did not hear the child's greeting.
4. The Cat is not speaking in Fifth Maow, though she
   has certainly been insulted.
5. Humans take a long time and learn nothing.
6. The child continues to greet the Cat, but the Cat
   continues washing her ear.

7 EXERCISE[10]

Carefully review the story at the beginning of the chapter, **mow
uh urrt pirp maow.** What Gentle Reproach was used? How

---

[10] No practical exercise with a native speaker is provided because of the danger inherent
in deliberately causing a Cat offense. However, you are sure to do so inadvertently.
Study the following chapter carefully.

many levels of the Ladder of Offense did the Cat experience and express? Did she jump any levels?

Why do you think the child ignored so many clear warnings? Notice that the adult, who clearly was within earshot, also ignored a direct complaint from the Cat. Why do you think that was?

What happened then? Was the Cat justified in its action? Is the adult or the child more at fault?

Discuss variously for a child's age of two and six years.

Chapter 9

APOLOGY

◆

SITUATIONAL USE OF THE VARIOUS
LEVELS OF APOLOGY

◆

THE SEAL OF APOLOGY

◆

THE FOLLOW-UP

ma` ruh maowpirp	To Err Is Human[1]
'awarra` meuh`a mRaow(c4) truh(c4)	Like a mule (on a treadmill), who only moves to grind (grain)
fru(a7) ma` ruh maowpirp meuh`a aaa`(c4)	A human does not speak without causing distress[2]
mow mowruh(d1) row. mow broh uh nbroh	The Cat is tolerant and forgiving and takes little notice[3]
maowpirp mboh uh 'aow mow m`mow(a1) maow nmiaow(a1)	The Cat takes no personal offense no matter how grievous the error
mow mowruh(d1) maow(a7) maow(d7) miaow	Cats must[4] however indiCate where error has occurred
mowrrah rir rro mbo	In order to promote learning
ma` ruh maowpirp nruh maow prih(d2) pirp uh prih(c4) mow nmbruuh	The worthy human gives ear and listens to Cat displeasure
fru(a7) truh(c4)	And mends (its grammar) accordingly

---

[1] This poem/prayer is taken from ancient Cat teaching tales.
[2] i.e., to Cats.
[3] Lit. "Mowlike, the Cat sees and does not see."
[4] "Cat nature compels"—this word may never be used by humans to indiCate a Cat duty. It is a grammatical error requiring a Level-Four apology.

VOCABULARY

'awarra`(b1)	mule
broh prip(b4)(C)	to look for, to seek
broh pirp(c4)(nC)	to look for, to seek
fru(a7)	thus, so, behold
ma` ruh maowpirp(f1)	human, "the non-Cat whose attribute is giving offense"
m`mow(a1) mow(d4) broh pirp[5] ma`rrah(f5)	to apologize for, in order to, for the sake of (nC)
maow(a7) maow(d7) miaow(b4)	to point out error, to speak from 2nd to 7th Maow
maow miaow(a1)(d1)	to take offense
maowpirp(f1)	error; offense-giving; sin
mowrrah(d1)	for, in order to, for the sake of (C)
mRaow(c4)(nC)	to walk, move
mrrrow(f4)	remorse
rir rro mbo	learning; arts and sciences
rir nrow(b4, c4)	to be ashamed
rrah(b3)	purpose, intention

[5] Lit. "to seek the Goddess through Cat Presence." Cats consider that a human who has erred has lost contact with Mow. Apology is not, therefore, primarily addressed to the Cat. The Cat is merely a conduit for access to Mow.

1 APOLOGY

In certain situations it is necessary for a human to apologize to a Cat. Students must familiarize themselves with all the levels both of the Offended Voice and of Apology. Study this chapter carefully.

RULES OF APOLOGY

1. When in doubt, apologize.

2. Follow your first apology with the Seal of Apology (see below).

3. Where there is no response from the Cat, repeat the apology, as many times as necessary, until you gain acceptance of the apology (the eating of the Seal).

4. In exceptional circumstances, a Cat may eat the Seal of Apology without actually accepting the apology.[6] This will usually be signaled by an Offended Blink after consumption of the Seal. This is called by Cats, "Digression" or "Digestion."

5. *Except after a Digression,* where it should be followed by repetition of the same level of apology, if the response at any point is an Offended Blink, proceed *immediately* to a higher level of apology.

---

[6] Usually when the Cat is particularly partial to the delicacy offered. In circumstances such as this, the gesture of eating should be seen as approving of the food *only.*

6. Any repetition of an offense, whether inadvertent or deliberate, requires the apology level immediately above the one previously accepted for that offense (i.e., a *second* unbracketed mention of another Cat will require a Third Level apology).

7. You may attempt three *levels* of apology on any particular occasion.[7] If your apology is then not accepted, make no more attempt to address the Cat until the Cat speaks to you.

8. Where an apology has not immediately been accepted, the occasion of the Cat next addressing you may be taken to be an acceptance of your apology even though this is not specifically mentioned.[8]

9. Remember the Cat adage, "True apology in a human is as rare as moderation in a flea," and strive to be the exception.

ORDINARY OR NONAPOLOGETIC APOLOGY

NMaow (Unoffended) is the level of ordinary, everyday apology, where no offense has been given and little taken, i.e., where a Cat has not used any Gentle Reproach or Offended Voice.

ma` nruh!   –   I didn't mean it! *or*

row(f 7) ma`   –   I am non-Cat

---

[7] Do not confuse the number of *levels* with the number of *repetitions*. You may make any number of repetitions of a particular level of apology, until and unless the Seal is accepted or you receive an Offended Blink in response.

[8] This is a true example of Cat magnanimity and not, as Hundfress suggests, a question of absent-mindedness.

are the equivalent of the English "Pardon me?" or "Pardon me!" and are used in very similar situations: i.e., where a human has not heard what a Cat has said or unwittingly touches or bumps into a Cat.

THE LEVELS OF APOLOGY

The Nine Levels of Apology may be roughly divided into three groups of three. The first three levels allow offending humans to exculpate themselves by pointing out that human genetic deficiency or experiential-based dysfunction may be the real source of the offense. Effectively they serve as gentle reminders to the Cat that a human is a human and not a Cat, and therefore, not much can be expected of you.[9] This is not unlike the general level of human to human apology.

1. **ma` ruh maowpirp row(f 7)!**   – I'm only human!

2. **ma` ruh maowpirp nrrow!**   – It's not my fault I'm so insensitive! (lit. I am/ humans are whiskerless)

---

[9] In cosmic terms, the fault is transferred to Mow.

3. **mow(d4) m`ma` ruh**   – It's not my fault I can't
    maowpirp prih   remember things!
    'aow prip(d1)!   (lit., Mow has given
                        me/humans flat ears)

The second three levels admit individual culpability. These apologies are based on the idea that *certain actions fall within the scope of individual human control.* At these levels you take responsibility for your own actions. This is a difficult concept for humans, but with time and repetition you may become accustomed to the attitude.

4. **ma` pra urr(c4)**   I chose unwisely, but I
    nmowruh(a3) muh ar   will improve.[10]
    bRuh mowruh(a3).

5. **mrrrow(f4) mboh mboh** – It is with enormous remorse
    mboh muh mboh   that I recognize having
    maow(f1) mboh   offered great insult to you.
    mboh pra pirp m`mow.   Please forgive me. (lit. But
    muh mow row.   you are Cat.)

---

[10] Literally, "but my intention is to desire Mowlikeness." Cats believe that most, if not all transgressions above a certain level betoken a failure of intent; they do not accept (or indeed understand) the concept "weak-willed." If one had sincerely intended to improve, one would have improved. Therefore the promise you make here is *to have the intention* to improve. Again, a difficult but not impossible concept for most humans.

6. **ma` ruh maowpirp ruh**   – My error is arrogance, and I
   'awaruh row(a1)   do not understand my
   mowruh(a1) **rowmiow**   relative value in the
   (c4) **uh ma`**[11] **nmeow**   scheme of things. Please
   (c4) **muh ma` nme**(a2)   teach me. (lit. Cat leads
   m`mow(d4). **mow**(a1)   non-Cat to Mow.)
   m`mow**(d4) **ma`
   miaow(a1).

The highest three levels of apology rely upon self-abasement as an encouragement to forgiveness. Note the use of the Flattery Voice.

7. **ma` rir nrow, mrrew**   – I am ashamed. Even my
   ruh ma` rir nrow   name is covered in
   muh mow(a1)   shame. But you are the
   brroh ruh mow(d4).   shadow of Mow.

8. **mRRew**(a3) **nmah^, aw** – My face is dirty, my paws
   nmah^, mrrew ow   are dirty, my name is dirt
   nmah^ ow ow row   itself. But Cat is incapable
   muh mow nbroh   of seeing filth.[13]
   nmah.[12]

---

[11] The personal pronoun is naturally *never* omitted from an apology. There can be no such thing as apology in the passive voice.

[12] This word may not take the Flattery Voice.

[13] I.e., because she is too pure.

9. nb'row nmah nrrow   – My blasphemous violation[14]
   nmrrew awarrobra(c4)   is of unforgivable magni-
   ma` mboh mboh   tude and only one of
   mboh 'awaruh(f3) muh   your magnanimous bear-
   m<u>ow</u>r<u>uh</u>(d1) mow(a1)   ing, great intelligence,
   m<u>ow</u>r<u>uh</u> m<u>ow</u>r<u>uh</u>.   and goddesslike abilities
                               could even listen to a
                               request for absolution.

2 SITUATIONAL USE OF THE VARIOUS LEVELS OF APOLOGY

The following lists are by no means comprehensive. They are given here as guidance only, in an effort to make the student familiar with the Cat attitude to offences. There are many, many more ways of offending a Cat than could possibly be listed here. Even the assignment of levels to offenses can only be offered as a general guide, since individual Cats may take a greater or lesser[15] amount of offense from any particular error, depending on what they see as the offender's state of mind in the moment the offense was committed.

The following should be studied in conjunction with the section on the Offended Voice (see Chapter Eight).

---

[14] Dogfodder's alternative rendering of this term as "naked, unclean, whiskerless, dog-licking obscenity" has some virtue as far as literalness is concerned, but is long-winded and invidious, besides imparting an air of levity to what should be treated with the utmost seriousness. Students should put this translation out of their minds when apologizing at this level.
[15] Usually greater.

1. OFFENSES REQUIRING FIRST-LEVEL APOLOGY

These are normally indiCated by some form of preMaow reproach such as the Tail-Tip Twitch

❖ Minor grammatical solecisms, such as saying **ma`** too often where it may be omitted

❖ Relatively inconsequential errors in the Begin Note or Tonal Shape of simple words (Note: Confusions between Cat and non-Cat BNTS are *not* considered minor, see level 5)

❖ Volunteering unwanted information about yourself (e.g., "I'm tired today")

❖ Overuse of non-Cat adjectives and the adjectival breath

❖ Failure to respond to the Invitation to Intimacy

2. OFFENSES REQUIRING SECOND-LEVEL APOLOGY

Usually signaled by an Offended Blink without any speech

❖ Mention of a Cat who is not present, without the flattery bracket

❖ Causing of mild discomfort or irritation to the Cat, such as by failing to offer a flattering description or attention where appropriate

❖ Expressing high intent where it is grammatically inappropriate (i.e., without permission)

❖ Causing a Cat to move from a comfortable position

❖ Rushing or disturbing a Cat engaged in ritual

3. OFFENSES REQUIRING THIRD-LEVEL APOLOGY

Usually signaled by a communiCation in Second Maow

❖ Late or neglected mealtime
❖ Taking an unnecessary time over the preparation of the Cat's food offering at regular mealtimes (see below for other times)
❖ Redundancy or unnecessariness
❖ Use of Cat or perfect verbs with a non-Cat subject
❖ Failure to respond to a Cat's express desire for food, attention, or any service

4. OFFENSES REQUIRING FOURTH-LEVEL APOLOGY

Usually signaled by a communiCation in Second Maow accompanied by the Offended Blink

❖ Speaking to another human in Cat
❖ Too much discussion of other Cats; asking a Cat (too many) questions (one may be too many)[16]
❖ Attempting to use an extended Tonal Shape
❖ Making sucking or kissing noises to attract a Cat's attention instead of the grammatically appropriate approach

5. OFFENSES REQUIRING FIFTH-LEVEL APOLOGY

Generally accepted as a response to Third Maow complaints

❖ Expressing or feeling disapproval of a Cat
❖ Confusion of the C and nC BNTS

---

[16] But not when the questions relate to food preferences.

❖ Using a defective verb with a Cat subject
❖ Mistake in the Fantasy Voice Begin Note
❖ Taking an unnecessary time to produce a promised tid-bit (i.e., not the regular meal)

6. OFFENSES REQUIRING SIXTH-LEVEL APOLOGY

Generally accepted as a response to Fourth Maow complaints
❖ Inappropriate or too free use of the Cat's name
❖ Asking a Cat's Particular name
❖ Attempting to indiCate your own positive ownership of something with the word **m'ma`**
❖ Too free or inappropriate use of the word **mow**(d4)
❖ Attempting to use the imperative form of the verb to give an order to a Cat

7. OFFENSES REQUIRING SEVENTH-LEVEL APOLOGY

Generally accepted as a response to Fifth Maow
❖ Addressing a Cat as "non-Cat" (**ma`**)
❖ Using the address **mRaow** without subsequently offering food
❖ Using the true comparative or superlative to discuss the Cat
❖ Causing or allowing physical discomfort to a Cat in the first instance
❖ Persistent interference with a Cat engaged in ritual

❖ Inappropriate challenge or blatant disbelief where the Fantasy Voice may have been used by a Cat

8. OFFENSES REQUIRING EIGHTH-LEVEL APOLOGY

Generally accepted as a response to Sixth Maow

❖ Attempting to impose one's will on a Cat (i.e., forcing it to get off the bed or go outside)
❖ Using the Maow voice to indiCate annoyance with a Cat
❖ The use of the **'arra** form to ask a question
❖ Causing or allowing physical discomfort to a Cat after a direct complaint
❖ Use of the Fantasy Voice for humorous purposes at an inappropriate moment

9. OFFENSES REQUIRING NINTH-LEVEL APOLOGY

The appropriate response for Seventh Maow communiCation

❖ Using the **'arra** form to enquire into a Cat's name
❖ Causing or allowing pain or suffering to a Cat
❖ Using the verb "must" (**mupRup**) to a Cat
❖ Use of the Fantasy Voice to make an insincere offer of food in a misguided attempt at a joke

You will have noticed that the majority of offenses entail grammatical imprecision or inaccuracy. Remember that Cats are fiercely protective of their language. This is not a question of personal arrogance,[17] but of grammatical precision,[18] which Cats see as absolutely essential.

3 THE SEAL OF APOLOGY

Grammatical precision demands that all apologies be accompanied by an offering of food, preferably of a special or tidbit variety.[19] Otherwise, you risk being thought insincere. Except in cases of Digression, mentioned above, the accepting of the tidbit is an indiCation of forgiveness. The appropriate response to forgiveness is

ma` RRow – I am blessed

You will find that Cat forgiveness is complete. The Cat will not mention your offense again.

4 THE FOLLOW-UP

Acceptance of the apology should best be followed by a brief but intense session of Flattery Voice communiCation. The acceptance of such descriptive phrases offers the Cat further opportunity to indiCate that all is forgiven and indeed, forgotten.

---

[17] Dogfodder, in "The assumption of superiority as manifested in the language," *AJCS*, Vol. V, No. 3, pp. 261–90.

[18] The human explanation for the current problems of society as being caused by the breakdown of the family or of religion or by violence on television, while the matter of grammatical laxity, particularly in the English language, is entirely ignored, is laughed at by Cats. "Grammatical laxity is the root of all ill," is an ancient Cat proverb.

[19] And certainly not the Cat's regular meal.

fr<u>ah</u> mow(a1) ruh ma`row – your fur is just as black
  fr<u>ah</u> uh fr<u>ah</u>   as black![20]

mow(a1) m<u>owruh</u>(d1) row – how magnificently
                                       Mowlike you are!

5 COMPREHENSION EXERCISES

'awarra` ow mew(b1) ma` ruh maowpirp row. marro(a5) 'aaa muh mow nmeow(b4). ma` ruh maowpirp 'aaa b'row uh b'row muh 'aaa: *mow m`ma`* . . . ! mow(d4) m`mow(a1) mboh maaw(d4) mboh prip muh mow mowruh mrow. RRow ma`! nrowb row, nrrow, prih 'aow. fru(a7) mow mew m`mew maow pirp.

6 WRITTEN EXERCISE

1. As you (nC) speak, so shall you apologize (proverb).
2. Cat nature is forgiving (lit, Cat leads non-Cat to Mow).
3. I committed a dreadful error, but the Cat was magnanimous.
4. The Cat spoke in Second Maow and gave the Slow Blink.
5. The human was ashamed and apologized.

---

[20] Note that the phrase offered here may not be used indiscriminately with any Cat. Tailor your follow-up expressions to the Cat exactly as you would any Flattery Voice comment. Be imaginative!

7 PRACTICAL EXERCISES WITH A NATIVE SPEAKER

Eavesdrop the next time you hear the neighborhood Cats in debate. Can you understand the conversation? If not, try, as best you can, to take down what they say in writing. Ask your resident Cat to translate difficult terms. Be sure to preface each expression you repeat with the phrase, **mow meuh`a pra miaow**—"then a Cat said." Otherwise your Cat may forget that you are quoting, and take offense if the expression is, for example, grammatically inappropriate.

If the Cat nevertheless responds by taking offense at any point, do not engage in a fruitless attempt to remind her that the remarks are not your own. Simply reply with the correct level of apology.

PART TWO

Tonality

Chapter 10

TONALITY

◆

THE POINT SYSTEM

INTRODUCTION TO TONALITY

Like a number of human languages, such as Chinese and Thai, Cat is a tonal language. That is, the meaning of a communiCation is indiCated not entirely by the variation of consonants and vowels that compose it, but also by the tonal component, or intonation pattern. This sometimes happens in English, though it may not be consciously recognized by ordinary native speakers. For example, the meaning of the speech sounds that may be indiCated by the writing signs "Me?" and "Me!" are really quite different. Because what we think of as the central component—the me-ness of the communiCation—remains the same, it is easy to overlook the fact that the first may communiCate something like "Is it me you mean/want?" and the second "I am the one!" English and most other so-called nontonal languages frequently indiCate meaning through tone, so if you are a native speaker of any human language, your ear is somewhat prepared for the tonal factor that is a central meaning signifier in Cat.

Nevertheless, the extremely high degree to which tone affects meaning in Cat may make it the single most difficult feature for nonnative speakers. Almost every vowel–consonant cluster in Cat has a wide range of possible meanings according to both Tonal Shape and Begin Note: some clusters have as many as four hundred different meanings.

Fortunately, the use of both Tonal Shape and Begin Note is limited for ordinary conversation, and Seven Tonal Shapes and Six Begin Notes are sufficient for the beginner.

THE POINT SYSTEM

The Cat ear is a much finer instrument than its human counterpart. On the Cat scale our octave is more properly called an octogintuna,[1] signifying that there are eighty-one, rather than eight, notes making up the scale. These eighty-one notes are called **points** in English, to distinguish them from the tones and semitones of the Pythagorean scale. Each of the Pythagorean notes (do-re-mi-fa-so-la-ti-do) is a note within the octogintuna, but instead of being separated by one or two semi-tones, they are separated by up to ten points. It is difficult at first for the untrained human ear to distinguish between points, but over time and with persistence, you will find your ear acclimatizing.

[1] A human word that is particularly pleasing to Cats, as it carries connotations of both music and food, and suggests some of the richness of Cat, generally absent in human languages. Most words in Cat are much richer than the one-word English translation provides.

Chapter 11

THE TONAL SHAPES

◆

NOTATION DEVICES

TONAL SHAPE

The intonation pattern, called the Tonal Shape, may be thought of rather as a short passage of song, where a word or syllable runs over one or more notes. Compare, for example, the intonation patterns in the English *oh, really* meaning, "I see," with the same phrase when it means "How dare you!" and again, when it means, "I simply don't believe what you say." In the last example, one syllable may move over several notes.

In inter-Cat communiCations, the number of notes per syllable is unrestricted.[1] In what may be called the "human cluster" of Cat,[2] except for two Tonal Slides, the Tonal Shapes are restricted to no more than four notes on a syllable.[3]

In addition, in the human cluster, the tonal shape ranges generally over only two octaves. Using a Base Note[4] of Middle C, most humans will find all Tonal Shapes of the human cluster within their vocal range.

Tonal shapes are difficult at first. But take heart: you may be understood by a good-natured, well-fed Cat even if you make no distinction between points in a Tonal Shape.

---

[1] The highest number so far recorded is 546 points. Many of these are so close together that they are indistinguishable to the human ear.
[2] That is, the language presented in this book.
[3] Except for Extended Tonal Shapes, but these are used only by Cats.
[4] See below.

NOTATION DEVICES

A point is signaled by the sign #, a **double-point**[5] by *. The sign + indiCates movement up the scale, the sign - signifies movement down the scale. Where there is no change from the Begin Note or the preceding note the mark used is the sign =. Each movement is called a **shift**. The numbers signify the number of points or double-points occurring in the shift. Thus +3# -1* -6# indiCates a Tonal Shape shifting up three points from Begin Note, down one double-point, then down another six points.

NOTE: Where a word has more than one syllable, a shift may sometimes, but not always, indiCate where the syllabic change occurs.

THE 7 TONAL SHAPES

Practice and memorize these patterns. If possible, ask a Cat you know well for assistance.

1.   -3* -3* -3* -3* +3* +3* +3* +3*
2.   == +5# +4# -2* -2# +1* -3# -3# -1* +3*

---

[5] The double-point usually consists of two or three points.

3.   -4* +5* +3# +3* +2# +5# +1*

4.   === -3* -3* -2*=== +2* +3* +5*==

5.   ===== +4* +7* +2#

6.   -1# -1# -1# -1# -1# +1# +1# +1#

7.   ================[6]

---

[6] Sometimes called the "Bastard" Shape. Because, even in trunCation, this shape remains no more than the Begin Note repeated, it is not, properly speaking, a Tonal Shape at all. However, in action it is like a Tonal Shape and for ease is included here.

Chapter 12

TRUNCATION

◆

BEGIN-AND-END

◆

MIDDLE

◆

ALTERNATE

TRUNCATED TONAL SHAPE

Correct English speech, and that of many other human languages, allows for certain contractions. "I am" may become
"I'm," "do not" may be pronounced "don't." It is the same
with Cat. But here we are speaking, not of a contraction in
the consonant–vowel cluster, but in the musicality. That is,
in the Tonal Shape.

There are three forms of Tonal Shape trunCation: Begin-
and-End; Middle; and Alternate.

BEGIN-AND-END

This consists, as its name implies, of omitting the beginning and end of the Tonal Shape. Any number of notes
may be omitted, *but an equal number must be dropped
from the beginning and from the end.*

For example, Tonal Shape 2 in its entirety is, as we have
already seen,

$$== +5\# +4\# -2^* -2\# +1^* -3\# -3\# -1^* +3^*$$

In its trunCated form, an equal number of shifts may be
dropped from each end. If three are dropped, the Tonal
Shape then becomes

$$+4\# -2^* -2\# +1^* -3\#.$$

If four are dropped, the shape becomes

$$-2^* \ -2\# \ +1^*,$$

and so on.

MIDDLE

As its name implies, this is the opposite of Begin-and-End trunCation. Here the notes in the middle are omitted. Again, any number may be dropped, but they must come from the exact center of the shape.[1] Tonal Shape 2 might therefore become

$$== \ +5\# \ +4\# \ -2^* \ +1^* \ -3\# \ -3\# \ -1^* \ +3^*$$

or

$$== \ +5\# \ +4\# \ -3\# \ -3\# \ -1^* \ +3^*$$

or

$$== \ -1^* \ +3^*$$

but never

$$==-2^* \ -2\# \ +1^* \ -3\# \ -3\# \ -1^* \ +3^*.$$

ALTERNATE

Again the name indiCates the nature of the trunCation. Here alternate shifts are omitted from the pattern, always in

---

[1] It follows that, in an even-numbered Tonal Shape, only an even number may be omitted; in an odd-numbered, an odd number. But see Chatto, "Allowable irregularities in truncation" [*sic*], *JCAT*, Vol. 10, No. iii, pp. 116–41.

a regular pattern. The count may be begun from the first shift, or the first shift may count as the first omission. Thus, every other shift being omitted from TS2 would produce the shape

$$= +5\# -2^* +1^* -3\# +3^*$$

or

$$= + 4\# -2\# -3\# -1^*,$$

depending on whether the omission begins on the first or second shift; while omitting every third would produce

$$== +4\# -2^* +1^* -3\# -1^* +3^*$$

or

$$= +5\# -2^* -2\# -3\# -3\# +3^*.$$

Any pattern of omission may be adopted, so long as it is regularly maintained. Thus a trunCation pattern of three–one would produce the shape

$$+4\# -3\#$$

or

$$=-2^* -3\#,$$

depending on where the count begins.

Nonnative speakers may make use of trunCations, but beginners are advised to avoid them.

Chapter 13

EXTENSIONS

◆

EUPHONY

◆

THRENODY

◆

MAGNIFICAT

THE EXTENDED TONAL SHAPE

In English, in order to impress an audience with rhetoric, speakers may sometimes use larger, longer words. In particular, a speaker may call upon Latin cognates, those mellifluous, multisyllabic words that convince the credulous that one is eduCated. Thus, if we really wanted someone to leave us alone, we would tend to use the short and succinct, "Fuck off!" If, however, our real desire was to impress an opponent with our eloquence, we might use something closer to the schoolboy: "Remove yourself from our distinguished presence!" Often such usage is meant to be amusing.[1]

In a similar way, Cats have access to rhetorical length, but again, the length is added to the musicality rather than the vocabulary. This usage is called the Extended Tonal Shape. Any number of tones or points may be inserted between what are called the Touchstone Notes or individual points of the Basic Tonal Shape.

Nonnative speakers may not use any extended Tonal Shape. See Chapter Nine, Apology.

EUPHONY

This is a simple extension of the Basic Pattern by repeating each note in the pattern any number of times.

---

[1] Cats seldom use extended Tonal Shapes for purposes of amusement.

Tonal Shape 3, as we have seen above, has a Basic or Touchstone pattern

$$-4^* +5^* +3\# +3^* +2\# +5\# +1^*$$

This may be extended as

$$-4^*===+5^*===+3\#===+3^*===+2\#===+5\#===+1^*===$$

It is often used in singing.

THRENODY

This is created by the insertion of any pattern of notes repeating between the notes of the Basic Tonal Shape.

Tonal Shape 1 has the Basic or Touchstone pattern

$$-^*3 -^*3 -^*3 -^*3 +^*3 +^*3 +^*3 +^*3$$

Take the three-note pattern $-^*8 -^*3 +^*6,$[2] and add it between each of the notes of the basic shape. Thus

$$-^*3 -^*8 -^*3 +^*6 -^*3 -^*8 -^*3 +^*6 -^*3 -^*8 -^*3 +^*6 -^*3 -^*8 -^*3$$
$$+^*6 -^*3 -^*8-^*3 +^*6 +^*3 -^*8 -^*3 +^* +^*3 -^*8 -^*3 +^*6 +^*3 -^*8 -$$
$$^*3 +^*6 +^*3 \; [3]$$

---

[2] This is a commonly occurring Threnody pattern, but of course any three notes may be chosen.

[3] The Threnody may also be added at the beginning and end of the Basic Shape, but this form is less common.

This is sometimes used with enemies, to warn them of approaching personal disaster, or to make them aware of a hitherto unsuspected ancestry likely to have an effect on the outcome of the approaching battle. It is also used in territorial disputes.

THE MAGNIFICAT[4]

This extended shape may involve the addition of hundreds of notes to a Tonal Shape. There are many variations.[5] Generally the detail will be lost to the human ear, but the intent of the communiCation is usually self-evident. It is rare for a Cat to sing the MagnifiCat in the presence of humans.

REPEATS

Extended Tonal Shapes may be extended further through the use of compliCated repeats and slides, but this is beyond the scope of this book. Most Cats do not make use of complex extended Tonal Shapes with nonnative speakers.

---

[4] Or "Inspired Shape".

[5] Feldmaus has suggested that every Cat may have an individual MagnifiCat Pattern, which constitutes the Cat "fingerprint." This is an extremely interesting idea, and well worth research. See "Tonal Shape extensions as voiceprint," CK Vol 5, No. ii, where she also suggests there may be a link between the individual MagnifiCat and the ineffable name. This seems unlikely.

Chapter 14

THE BEGIN NOTES

◆

BEGIN NOTE AND MEANING

THE BEGIN NOTES

A Begin Note is just what it says: it is the musical note or tone on which the word *begins.* Although altogether more than forty-six Begin Notes exist in Cat, as mentioned above, for purposes of conversation with humans they may be limited to six. In addition, these range over only one octogintuna, and are therefore accessible to all humans. In Classical Cat, they are called the Six Begin Notes.[1] The Six Begin Notes and the language structured around them are traditionally said to have been deliberately designed for use with humans. Although some modern Cat theorists now dispute this,[2] it is a compelling explanation for the curious phenomenon of the "cluster" pattern, whereby a large number of simplified ideas can be expressed within the confines of those sounds capable of being reproduced by humans. If, for example, humans were to develop a language of communiCation between ourselves and apes, we would be likely to choose words with many clicks and plosives, since that would suit the vocal apparatus of the ape; and we would first develop words, such as "banana" and "scratch," which expressed concepts interesting to apes. In a similar

---

[1] Sometimes mistakenly called "The Vulgar Begin Notes." This idea has arisen through a misreading. The word is **meuh** (a3) (six), not **ma`uh** (f 7) (corrupt, vulgar, human).

[2] For example Dogfodder, "The vulgar notes—use or abuse?" *KS*, Winter 1996, in which the author suggests that far from being designed for comprehension by humans, the Six are simply what Cats consider "a crude area of sound." According to this theory, the fact that they are also the normal range for human voices is at best, coincidental, and at worst, a commentary on Cats' attitudes toward human beings.

way, Cats have limited the musicality of their language to
the human vocal apparatus.[3]

THE SIX BEGIN NOTES

The Begin Notes given here are for human use; in Cat use they
may vary. The Base or Central Note is Middle C. Remember
that the use of the first six letters of the alphabet is for conve-
nience only. These letters do not represent the musical notes.

a – Middle C or Base Note
b – 3 double-points above a
c – 3 double-points below a
d – 9 points above a
e – 4 points above a
f – 13 points below a

BEGIN NOTE AND MEANING[4]

Although much more research is needed on the subject
than what has so far been undertaken, it seems worthwhile
to mention here that, as far as can be seen, each of the six
(and perhaps each of the forty-six) Begin Notes carries a
general cluster of meaning. Until more is discovered of the
Cat worldview, some linkages will remain mysterious. But
the following may be of some assistance to the self-taught.

---

[3] The conceptual base of the language has been designed around our intellectual limitations.
[4] This is a brief survey only. For a fuller discussion of these see my *The Begin Note's Role in Meaning*, Bellew, 1988.

a — words that begin with Begin Note A seem to carry ideas of diversity and richness; birth, fertility; beauty and pleasure; age, wisdom, and death. Grammatically Begin Note A is mostly reserved for speech relating to Cats and food.

b — words denoting (Cat) action, including many verbs; concepts of vigor, positive attributes

c — words with a negative or neutral meaning, words denoting certain non-Cat action

d — carries overtones of oneness, indivisibility; divinity; particular, as opposed to general femaleness; cleanliness. The vibration of the D-note as a sound is said to include the vibration and thus the concepts of all the other notes except F. Thus the unity of D includes the diversity of A, and not vice versa. More research into the Cat worldview will undoubtedly makes such ideas clearer.

e — used in the Fantasy Voice

f — includes ideas of chaos and disruption; limitation; grammatically it is used in non-Cat verbs, nouns and pronouns, and may be considered the "opposite" or "completion" of Begin Note A[5]

---

[5] This is, however, not, as Dogfodder would have it, the "Negative Note." Anyone who imagines Cats consider chaos a negative has only to examine a bathroom after a Cat has been rearranging it.

Chapter 15

THE BASE NOTE

◆

ESTABLISHING THE BASE NOTE

◆

PURR NOTE AND BASE NOTE

THE BASE NOTE

Except for those speakers who have particularly deep or high voices, human students of the language should always use a Base Note of Middle C. However, Cats have widely different vocal ranges. Siamese, for example, tend to have rather deeper voices than Persians. The *interval* between the Begin Notes will always be consistent, but the Base Note itself may vary from Cat to Cat. The Cat's Base Note will then take the place of Middle C in the chart on page 142, and all the other Begin Notes must be taken *in relation to the Base Note.*

ESTABLISHING THE BASE NOTE

The Mow Method It is necessary to establish the Base Note of any individual Cat before communiCation can take place. This may usually be achieved by listening attentively when the Cat greeting **mow**(a1) is pronounced, since, because of its context, this greeting can never be confused with any other word. **The Begin Note of mow(a1) is the Cat's Base Note.** By referring to the chart, the student will be able to place the other Begin Notes in the speech of that particular Cat.[1]

---

[1] Self-taught students are advised to converse with one Cat only for the first few months of their studies. This refines the ear, and establishes an appreciation of the intervals between the Begin Notes. Students who speak to Cats with differing vocal ranges too early in their studies may find that their ear gets confused. Classroom teachers are advised not to bring more than one visiting Cat lecturer to the classroom during the first two terms of study.

PURR NOTE AND BASE NOTE

An alternative method of establishing a Cat's Base Note has recently been suggested, which may be useful for some students. It is not effective with all Cats, and the student is advised to be cautious in applying this method.

First, find the Purr Note.[2] This note, like the Base Note, varies from Cat to Cat. Since a purr is usually a blend of eleven notes ranging over one tone, care must be taken to establish the *lowest* note of the purr. Count fifteen double-points up from the Purr Note, then one point down. This method is successful with highly contented, unassuming Cats. It may not be used with most Siamese, whose voices, as mentioned above, tend to be deeper in relation to the Purr Note, and who anyway are rarely contented or unassuming. Use the Mow Method for establishing the Base Note of any Cat with a deep speaking voice.

[2] This method is not recommended for use with Cats who have a very breathy or asthmatic purr, as the Purr Note may be difficult to establish.

Appendix A

In Chapter 3 you read "The Story of The Story of BRRow and 'Aa" in Cat. Here is an English version of this famous Cat legend.

THE STORY OF BRROW AND 'AA

BRRow liked to play tricks from an early age. He had eight sisters and was always playing tricks on them and his mother. One night when BRRow was sleeping after a day of tricks, 'Aa, his sister, took his testicles from him. She placed them on her own eating dish. In the morning, she said to BRRow, "I have hunted and found some very tasty delicacies. Do not eat them, for they are only for me."

BRRow went to 'Aa's eating dish and ate up what he found there. 'Aa saw that the dish was empty. She laughed. "You think you have tricked me," she said.

BRRow cleaned his sexual parts in satisfaction after his meal. When he discovered that he had no testicles, he understood how 'Aa had tricked him. He laughed. He said, "That is an excellent trick. Now I will trick others until I have played a trick as good as the one 'Aa has played on me."

BRRow never sired any kittens; but every kitten born has
one hair from BRRow's pelt somewhere on her body.[1] In
this way BRRow is still playing tricks, and he will do so
until he has invented a better trick than the one 'Aa played
on him.

That is why, when a Cat has played a trick, he says,
BRRow.[2]

---

[1] Often on the forehead or around the ears. The loCation of this BRRow hair may sometimes be established through the fact that, as might be expected, it is a spot that needs
frequent gentle scratching. Some Cats say that when humans are stroking or scratching
a Cat, they are "hunting the BRRow spot."

[2] This sound is the equivalent of the English "Ha Ha." Some say that whenever a Cat
laughs, it is because any joke reminds her of the "First Joke": the trick 'Aa played on
BRRow. Cats sometimes laugh when a human finds their BRRow hair.

Appendix B

Translations

CHAPTER ONE

The Cat. The Cat is pretty. You (C) are hungry. The food is cold. The whiskers are wet.

CHAPTER TWO

Milk is nice. Wet fur is not nice. The little Cat has a small tail. You (nC) must make an offering of milk.

CHAPTER THREE

Your food is in the bowl. The salmon is swimming in the water. I (C) want food. At night the Cat hunted and in the morning she played a trick and laughed.

CHAPTER FOUR

You really are a very pretty Cat. You (C) have a discerning eye and you saw the mouse. Was the mouse's tail especially delicious? It was certainly tasty.

CHAPTER FIVE

You are at rest on my lap. You have been decorating the bathroom. Now you are kneading my knee. Meanwhile I am stroking your fur. You are going to commune with heaven (go to sleep).

CHAPTER SIX

Are you a white Cat without markings? You (nC) must use your eyes better. I am a white Cat with blue eyes and six black hairs on my occiput. The adorable kittens are asleep in the basket. Here is a toy.

CHAPTER SEVEN

Does non-Cat (do you) believe that a Cat's whisker is lucky? I'm sorry, I (nC) didn't quite catch that. There is a canary eating from your dish (joke)! Although it is raining, the Cats are debating in the garden. It was a dark and stormy night.

CHAPTER EIGHT

This child is stupid. The Cat has delivered three Early Warnings. Now the Cat is speaking in Second Maow. The (adult) human is not listening. Does the human have ears? Oh, yes, the human has ears. What a pity it does not use them.

CHAPTER NINE

Mules are better than humans. They only say one thing and no one understands it. Humans say anything they like and then try to shift the blame. Mow has given Cats an onerous task but they undertake it with cheerful determination. Poor humans! They have no tail, no whiskers, and flat ears. No wonder they offend Cats all day long.

Lexicon

CAT–ENGLISH

'a(a7)	if
'aa(d1)	'Aa (name)
'aa(c7)	on, in
'aiou(a4)	bed, basket, washtub, drawer
'aow(b1)	little, small; flat, not pointed (of ears)
'arra(a7)	question signifier
'aw(c4)(nC)	to continue a displeasing act
'awarra`(b1)	mule
'awaruh(f3)	sin, crime, mistake, error
'Rowow(d2)	pretty
'RRaow(a2)	lonely
^ra`(b1)	toy
^ow(f4)(nC)	skin; jeans, pants, trousers; clothes
a`bRah(b1)	bathroom
aaa`(c4)(nC)	to squeak, say
ar(a1)	intention, will; future indiCator
arp(b4, c4)	to run, scurry
arruh(a5)	future, the future
aw(c3)	paw, foot, hand
awa(f 7)	dog
berah(a1, f 7)	to like
b'row(d1)	hair

b'row(d1) **uh b'row**	"hairs of," i.e., many, numerous, uncountable
birr(b1)	cushion, pillow
birr(b5)	milk
birr(b5) **birr**	cream
bra(c4)(nC)	to work; lift, carry, fetch; do
braa`(f 7)(nC)	to sit
brap(b4, c4)	to eat
breh(b2)	tree
breh(c2)	fence, wall
broh(a4)	eye
broh(b4, c4)	to see
broh prip(b4)(C)	to look for, to seek
broh pirp(c4)(nC)	to look for, to seek
broh(b4) **uh nbroh** (b4)(C)	to "look and not look"; i.e., to blink at, give the Offended Blink
brroh(a1)	admiringly, in admiration
brroh(d4)	shadow
bRRow(d1)(C)	BRRow, the Trickster (name)
brrow(d1)(C)	white Cat with blue eyes, six black hairs on the occiput
bRRow(a1, f 7)	to laugh
bRRow(a6)	joke, trick
bRRow(b4)(C)	to play tricks
bRuh(b4, c4)	to wish, desire, need, want
bru(d2)(C)	white Cat, no markings

frah(d4)   dark, black

friuh(d2)(C)   black Cat with white nose, breast
                               and three paws, the right fore
                               black

fru(a7)   accordingly, so, thus, as

iow(a7)   or, otherwise; alternatively

iow(f4)(nC)   skin; paws, clothes; jeans

irr(a5)   delicious

m'   possessive marker

m'aaw(b4)(C)   to fight, to engage in (noble) battle;
                               to wrestle; to fight playfully or in
                               a spirit of sportsmanship

m'ow(b2)   softly, gently

m'ow(d1)   dinner, meal

m`   to, for, at, from, off, etc.

m`mow(a1) **mow**(d4)
  broh pirp   to apologize

ma` RRow(a1)(nC)   thank you

ma`row(b3)   coat/fur

ma`rrah(f5)   for, in order to, for the sake of (nC)

ma`(f 7) **ruh**
  maowpirp(f1)   human being, "the non-Cat whose
                               attribute is giving offense"

ma`uh(f 7)   corrupt, vulgar; human

maa`row(f 7)(nC)   to sing

maaa(a4)   floor

maaow(b4, c4)   to place, put

maaw(d4)(C)	task, divinely assigned duty/responsibility
maaw(f 7)(nC)	job, work, activity
mah(b4, c4)	to leave, depart; vaCate
mah(f 7)	really, quite; an expression of marginal interest or response to unsolicited information
maor(a5)	artist's material; paper; toilet paper
maow(b4, c4)	to come, walk, move forward
maow(a7) **miaow**(b4)	to speak in Second Maow
maow(c7) **miaow**(b4)	to speak in Fifth Maow
maow(d4)	song
maow(f1)	offense
maow pirp(c4)(nC)	to offend, insult
maowr(a2, a4)	salmon (flesh)
maowro(b4)(C)	to sing
marr(a5)	canary; bird with strong, interesting odor
marro(a5)	thing, object, idea, place
mawrow(b6)	door
mboh(c5)	big
mbruh(b5)	nice, pleasant
mbruuh(a5)	pleased
mbruuh(d1, a1)(C)	to be pleased with, to approve
me`a(a7)	first; now
meow(b4, c4)	to understand, accept
meow(d1)	today

meow(d4)	good, sharp, clear
merah(b4)	house
merowwap(a1, f 7)	to be hungry
meuh`a(a7)	second; then; afterward; meanwhile; while
meuh(d4)	numbers
mew(b4)(C)	to decorate, rearrange, sculpt; to pull
mew(a4)	(in the) morning
mew(b1)	good
mew(c7)	cold
mew(d4)	night, at night
mew(d4) **m'mew**(a4)	for a long time, "from night till morning"
mi'ao(a4)	garden
miaow(b4)(C)	to talk, say
miaow(a1)(C)	to guide, lead (by example)
mieh(d1)	delicate, dainty, refined; delicately, etc.
micw(a2, a4)	tuna (flesh)
miow(b4, c4)	to think, imagine, dream
miow(E1)	fantasy, imagining, thought
mir(d1)	claw, claws
mirr(c4)(nC)	to purchase, bring for approval, buy
moh(a5)	yes; indeed?
moh(a5) **row**(a1, f 7)	to believe (be in a state of belief)
mor(d1)	perfume, incense

moreh(c4)(nC)	to put down
morih(c4)(nC)	to pick up
morh(b4, c4)	to bite
mow(a1)	
mbruuh(a1)(C)	thank you
mow(a1)	Cat, Cat Presence, Higher Being
mow(b4)(C)	to accept an offering to Mow; to eat
mow(b3)	good
mowmew(d2)	kitten(s)
mowrow(c4)	winning, lucky
mowrrah(d1)	for, in order to, for the sake of (C)
mowruh(a3)	good, well-behaved, wise
mowruh(d3)	adorable, worthy of adoration/worship
mowruh(a1)	
rowmiow(c4)(nC)	to be arrogant, to put on airs, to act as if one were a Cat
mowruh(a5)	secret; secretly; Catlike
mowruh(b4)	quick, fast, quickly; Catlike
mowruh(d1)	majestic; majestically; Catlike
mra'(b4)(C)	to continue, carry on; carry out (usu. ritual)
mrah(d1)(C)	cream-colored Cat with dark nose, paws and tail tip
mrah(d2)(C)	gray Cat, no markings
mrah(d4)(C)	tabby Cat, no white markings

mRaow(b3)	food
mRaow(c4)(nC)	to walk, move
mraow(b4, c4)	to hunt
mrow(d1, b4)(C)	do, take, make
mRRah(a3)	money
mRRah(a4)	tidbit, snack
mRRaow(a3)	testicles
mRReh(a3)	face
mrrew(f 7)	name (nC)
mRRow(b4)(C)	to sleep, to commune with Mow
mrrrow(d4)	anger, displeasure; sorrowful anger
mrrrow(f4)	remorse, regret, sorrow
mrruh(d3)	name (C)
mruh(d4)(C)	ginger Cat, no white markings
muah(c3)	ticket
muh(a7)	when, nevertheless, and, but, however, who, which, etc.; the subordinate connector
mut(b7)(C)	pay attention! listen up!
nmbruh(f 7)	unpleasant
nme(a2)	nothing, zero, less than one; fraction
nmow(a1)	no one, nobody
nr'mow(a1)	there
nrow(c4) **rrow**(b3)(nC)	"to have no whiskers," to be stupid, to beg pardon for not hearing
owuh(c4)(nC)	to pull, squeeze, cause irritation to

pirp(c4)(nC)	to bring; offer, make an offering to
pra(c7)	already
pra^(b7)	sofa, firm claw sharpener
praow(c4)(nC)	to swim
preh(c1)	quickly, hastily
prih(b4, c4)	to hear
prih(d2)	ear
prip(b4)(C)	to give, bestow, vouchsafe; to accept, approve
prrew(a2, a4)	mouse(meat)
prruh(b4)(C)	to rest, recline; to grace; to be at ease
pwah(a1)(C)	to dislike, disdain
pwah(c3)	wet
pwah(f 7)	water
r'mow(a1)	here
rir(d4)	music
rir nrow(b4, c4)	to be ashamed
row(a1, f 7)	to be
Row(a4)	bowl, dish
row(b4, c4)	to have
Row^(b1)	lap, knee
rowb maar(b4, d1)(C)	to be angry, to storm, to lash one's tail
rowb(b6)	tail
rrah(b3)	purpose, intention, reason
rrah(c4)(nC)	to work, do

rro(b4, c4)	to wash, clean
rro(d4)	cleanliness
rrobra(c4)(nC)	to lick; to clean with water or other substance
rromiaow(b4)(C)	to lick, to clean with the tongue
RRooww(a1, d1)(C)	to purr
RRow(c6)	oversight, error; My Goodness! or What a pity!
rrow(b4)	whiskers
RRow(f 7)	poor, sad, pitiful
RRow(d1, a1)	to bless
RRuh(a5)	virtuous
rrup	"invitation to intimacy"
ruh(a1, f 7)	to intend, mean
ruh(a7)	like, similar to
ruh(b2)	with, by means of
Rup(c4)(nC)	to stroke, worship through caress
trrow(b1)	curtains, ladder, soft claw sharpener
truh(b4, c4)	to stir, mix, prepare; improve upon, adjust, knead, decorate; scratch; sharpen
uh(a7)	and, also
uh(f 7)	but
urr(b4, c4)	to choose
urrt(f 7)	child, offspring, cub (nC)
waa`(c4)(nC)	to scrap, squabble, wrangle
wah(d1)	handsome

ENGLISH–CAT

'Aa(name)	**'aa**
accept an offering to Mow; to eat (C) *v.*	**mow**(b4)
accordingly, so, thus, as *a.*	**fru**(a7)
admiringly, in admiration *a.*	**brroh**(a1)
adorable, worthy of adoration/worship	**mowruh**(d3)
already *a.*	**pra**(c7)
and, also	**uh**(a7)
anger, displeasure; sorrowful anger *n.*	**mrrrow**(d4)
apologize (nC) *v.*	**m`mow**(a1) **mow**(d4) **broh pirp**(c4)
arrogant, to be	**mowruh**(a1) **rowmiow** (c4)(nC)
artist's material; paper; toilet paper *n.*	**maor**(a5)
bathroom *n.*	**a`bRah**(b1)
basket	**'aiou**
be *v.*	**row**(a1)(f 7)
bed	**'aiou**(a4)
be pleased with, approve (C) *v.*	**mbruuh**(d1)(a1)
be angry, to storm, to lash one's tail (C) *v.*	**rowb maar**(b4, d1)
be ashamed *v.*	**rir nrow**(b4, c4)
believe (be in a state of belief) (C) *v.*	**moh**(a5) **row**(a1, f 7)

big *a.*	**mboh**(c5)
bite *v.*	**morh**(b4, c4)
black, dark *a.*	**frah**(d4)
blink at, forgive (C) *v.*	**broh**(b4) **uh** **nbroh**(b4)
bowl, dish *n.*	**Row**(a4)
bring; offer, make an offering to (nC) *v.*	**pirp**(c4)
BRRow, the Trickster(name)	**bRRow**(d1)(C)
canary; bird *n.*	**marr**(a5)
Cat, Cat Presence, Higher Being	**mow**(a1)
child, offspring, cub (nC) *n.*	**urrt**(f 7)
choose *v.*	**urr**(b4, c4)
claw, claws *n.*	**mir**(d1)
cleanliness *n.*	**rro**(d4)
clothes	**^ow**(f4)
coat, fur *n.*	**ma`row**(b3)
cold *a.*	**mew**(c1)
come, walk, move forward *v.*	**maow**(b4, c4)
continue, carry on, carry out (usu. ritual)(C) *v.*	**mra'**(b4)
continue a displeasing act (nC) *v.*	**'aw**(c4)
corrupt, vulgar	**ma`uh**(f 7)
cream *n.*	**birr**(b5)**birr**(b5)
crime *n.*	**'awaruh**(f3)
curtains, ladder, soft claw sharpener *n.*	**trrow**(b1)

cushion	**birr**(b1)
decorate, rearrange, sculpt; pull (C) *v.*	**mew**(b4)
delicate, dainty, refined; delicately *a.*	**mieh**(d1)
delicious *a.*	**irr**(a5)
dinner, meal *n.*	**m'ow**(d1)
dislike, disdain (C) *v.*	**pwah**(a1)
do, take, make (C) *v.*	**mrow**(d1, b4)
do (nC) *v.*	**bra**(c4)
dog *n.*	**awa**(f 7)
door *n.*	**mawrow**(b6)
ear *n.*	**prih**(d2)
eat *v.*	**brap**(b4, c4), **mow**(b4)(C)
eye *n.*	**broh**(a4)
face *n.*	**mRReh**(a3)
fantasy, imagining, thought *n.*	**miow**(E1)
fence	**breh**(c2)
fight, engage in (noble) battle; wrestle; fight playfully (C) *v.*	**m'aaw**(b4)
first, now *a.*	**me`a**(a7)
flat, not pointed (of ears) *a.*	**'aow**(b1)
floor *n.*	**maaa**(a4)
food *n.*	**mRaow**(b3)
for a long time *a.*	**mew**(d4) **m`mew**(a4)
for, in order to (C)	**mowrrah**(d1)

for, in order to (nC)   ma`rrah(f5)

fraction *n.*   nme(a2)

future, the future *n.*   arruh(a5)

garden *n.*   mi'ao(a4)

give, bestow, vouchsafe; to accept,
  approve (C) *v.*   prip(c4)

good, well-behaved, wise *a.*   mowruh(a3)

good *a.*   mew(b1)

good *a.*   mow(b3)

good, sharp, clear *a.*   meow(d4)

guide, lead *v.*   miaow(a1)(C)

hair *n.*   b'row(d1)

handsome *a.*   wah(d1)

have *v.*   row(b4, c4)

hear *v.*   prih(b4, c4)

here   r'mow(a1)

house *n.*   merah(b4)

human being   ma`(f 7) ruh
    maowpirp(f1);
    ma`

hunger, be hungry *v.*   merowwap(a1, f 7)

hunt *v.*   mraow(b4, c4)

if   'a(a7)

intend, mean *v.*   ruh(a1, f 7)

intention, will   ar(a1)

invitation to intimacy   rrup

jeans, pants, trousers   ^ow(f4)

job, work, activity (nC) *n.*	**maaw**(f 7)
joke, trick *n.*	**bRRow**(a6)
kitten	**mowmew**(d2)
lap, knee *n.*	**Row^**(b1)
laugh *v.*	**bRRow**(a1, f 7)
leave, depart; vaCate *v.*	**mah**(b4, c4)
lick, to clean with the tongue (C) *v.*	**rromiaow**(b4)
lick; to clean with water or other substance (nC) *v.*	**rrobra**(c4)
lift, carry, fetch (nC) *v.*	**bra**(c4)
like, similar to *a.*	**ruh**(a7)
like (C) *v.*	**berah**(a1, f 7)
little, small *a.*	**'aow**(b1)
lonely *a.*	**'RRaow**(a2)
look for, seek (C) *v.*	**broh prip**(b4)
look for, seek (nC) *v.*	**broh pirp**(c4)
majestic; majestically; Catlike *a.*	**mowruh**(d1)
many, numerous *a.*	**b'row**(d1) **uh b'row**
milk *n.*	**birr**(b5)
mistake, error *n.*	**'awaruh**(f3)
money *n.*	**mRRah**(a3)
morning, in the morning *a.*	**mew**(a4)
mouse (meat) *n.*	**prrew**(a2, a4)
mule	**'awarra`**
music *n.*	**rir**(d4)
name (nC) *n.*	**mrrew**(f 7)
name (C) *n.*	**mrruh**(d3)

nice, pleasant *a.*	**mbruh**(b5)
night, at night *a.*	**mew**(d4)
no one, nobody (C) *n.*	**nmow**(a1)
nothing, zero, less than one *n.*	**nme**(a2)
numbers *n.*	**meuh**(d4)
offend, insult *v.*	**maow**(f1)
	pirp(c4)(nC)
offense, insult *n.*	**maow**(f1)
on, in	**'aa**(c7)
open *v.*	**bra**(c4)
or, otherwise: alternatively	**iow**(a7)
oversight, error; My Goodness! or What a pity!	**RRow**(c6)
paw, foot, hand *n.*	**aw**(c3)
pay attention!, listen up!	**mut**(b7)(C)
perfume, incense *n.*	**mor**(d1)
pick up *v.*	**morih**(c4)(nC)
pillow	**birr**(b1)
place, put *v.*	**maaow**(b4, c4)
play tricks (C) *v.*	**bRRow**(b4)(C)
pleased *a.*	**mbruuh**(a5)
poor, sad, pitiful *a.*	**RRow**(f 7)
pretty *a.*	**'Rowow**(d2)
pull, squeeze, cause irritation to (nC) *v.*	**owuh**(c4)
purchase, bring for approval, buy (nC) *v.*	**mirr**(c4)

purpose, reason *n.*	**rrah**(b3)
purr (C) *v.*	**RRooww**(a1, d1)
put down *v.*	**moreh**(c4)(nC)
quick, fast, quickly; Catlike *a.*	**mowruh**(b4)
quickly, hastily	**preh**(c1)
really, quite	**mah**(f 7)
remorse, regret, sorrow *n.*	**mrrrow**(f4)
rest, recline, to grace, to be at ease (C) *v.*	**prruh**(b4)
run, scurry *v.*	**arp**(b4, c4)
salmon (fish) *n.*	**maowr**(a2)
salmon (meat) *n.*	**maowr**(a4)
scrap, squabble, wrangle (nC) *v.*	**waa`**(c4)
second; then; afterward; meanwhile; while *a.*	**meuh`a**
secret; secretly; Catlike *a.*	**mowruh**(a5)
see (C) *v.*	**broh**(a1)
see (nC) *v.*	**broh pirp**(c4)
shadow *n.*	**brroh**(d4)
sin *n.*	**'awaruh**(f3)
sing (C) *v.*	**maowro**(b4)
sing (nC) *v.*	**maa`row**(f 7)
sit (nC) *v.*	**braa`**(f 7)
skin (nC)	**^ow**(f4)
skin, clothes (nC) *n.*	**^ow**(f4)
sleep, commune with Mow (C) *v.*	**mRRow**(b4)
sofa, firm claw sharpener *n.*	**pra^**(b7)

softly, gently *a.*	**m'ow**(b2)
song *n.*	**maow**(d4)
speak in Fifth Maow (C) *v.*	**maow**(c7) **miaow**
speak in Second Maow (C) *v.*	**maow**(a7) **miaow**
squeak, say (nC) *v.*	**aaa`**(c4)
stir, mix, prepare; improve upon, adjust, knead, decorate; scratch; sharpen *v.*	**truh**(b4, c4)
stroke, worship through caress (nC) *v.*	**Rup**(c4)
stupid, to be; to beg pardon for not hearing (nC) *v.*	**nrow**(c4) **rrow**(b3)
swim, *v.*	**praow**(c4)(nC)
tail *n.*	**rowb**(b6)
take, *v.*	**marow**(c4)(nC)
talk, say (C) *v.*	**miaow**(b4)
task, divinely assigned duty/ responsibility (C) *n.*	**maaw**(d4)
testicles *n.*	**mRRaow**(a3)
thank you (nC)	**ma` RRow**(a1)
thank you (C)	**mow**(a1) **mbruuh**(a1)
there *a.*	**nr'mow**(a1)
thing, object, idea, place *n.*	**marro**(a5)
think, imagine, dream *v.*	**miow**(b4, c4)
ticket *n.*	**muah**(c3)
tidbit, snack *n.*	**mRRah**(a4)
to, for, at, from, off, etc.	**m`**

today *a.*   **meow**(d1)

toy *n.*   **^ra`**(b1)

tree *n.*   **breh**(b4)

tuna (fish) *n.*   **miew**(a2)

tuna (meat) *n.*   **miew**(a4)

understand, accept *v.*   **meow**(b4, c4)

unpleasant *a.*   **nmbruh**(f 7)

virtuous *a.*   **RRuh**(a5)

walk, move, *v.*   **mRaow**(c4)(nC)

wash, clean *v.*   **rro**(b4, c4)

washtub   **'aiou**(a4)

water, *n.*   **pwah**(f7)

wet *a.*   **pwah**(c3)

when, nevertheless, and, but,
  however, who, which, etc.;
  the subordinate connector   **muh**(a7)

whiskers *n.*   **rrow**(b4)

winning, lucky *a.*   **mowrow**(c4)

wish, desire, need, want *v.*   **bRuh**(b4, c4)

with, by means of   **ruh**(b2)

work, do (nC) *v.*   **bra**(c4)

yes; indeed?   **moh**(a5)